A PRIVATE
HISTORY OF
HAPPINESS

George Myerson has written a number of books
on ancient and contemporary culture, modern
thought, and the philosophy of everyday life.
He holds a PhD in English from Cambridge
University, and was for many years Lecturer and
Reader in English at King's College London.

A PRIVATE HISTORY OF HAPPINESS

NINETY-NINE MOMENTS OF JOY FROM AROUND THE WORLD

GEORGE MYERSON

HEAD
of ZEUS

First published in the United States in 2012 by Bluebridge,
an imprint of United Tribes Media Group Inc., New York

Published in the UK in 2013 by Head of Zeus Ltd

9 7 5 3 1 2 4 6 8

A CIP catalogue record for this book is available from the British Library.

ISBN (HB) 9781781854822
ISBN (E) 9781781854815

Printed in Germany

Text design by Cynthia Dunne

Head of Zeus Ltd
Clerkenwell House

Contents

Nature

Food and Drink

Well-Being

Creativity

Love

Evening

Introduction

We can immediately tell when someone is happy. It shows in their eyes and becomes, at that instant, their presence in the world.

In the pages that follow, there are ninety-nine moments of happiness. Each was experienced by an individual at a specific time—a few minutes, an hour, one particular day—ranging from over four thousand years ago to the recent past. These were women and men, young and old, of various backgrounds. They lived (or traveled) in many parts of the world, including North America and Britain; Continental Europe and China; North Africa, India, and Japan. They were on city streets or by rural rivers, in gardens or on mountaintops, in cottages or mansions, on long journeys or short breaks when they had these varied moments of color and sensation, understanding and peace, contact and laughter.

These everyday experiences of happiness have remained vivid and recognizable across the centuries, even millennia. They come naturally into focus, making lives that might otherwise seem distant feel intuitively understandable. Many of these joyful moments belong to diaries, which in different forms have been kept by people since the dawn of writing. Others are from letters, another form of personal chronicles of passing time. A few were written as poems, usually rather private works. Even in the case of well-known individuals, these are generally words from their quieter side.

These focused glimpses of other lives and times add up to a bigger idea. They bring real human happiness before our eyes. We can see here the potential for joy hidden inside ordinary life. This is a surprising and renewing effect in our own complex and high-pressure time. For many of us in the twenty-first century, happiness has become a riddle, a goal that remains strangely nebulous. Politics and economics, education and psychology all have happiness as their promise or end. But we need to grasp the happiness that is a strand of everyday life if we are to make good on any of these promises. If we look at the statistics, we are, in industrialized societies, in general wealthier and healthier than our ancestors—but are we happier?

Like seeing colors or hearing a tune, feeling happy is different for each of us and in every experience. It is a sensation in the air, a depth to the horizon. These moments of joy from the past resonate and echo, prompting positive reflection. They invite us to think about particular people's experiences of being happy and not merely about generalities or clichés or abstract puzzles that seem to need solving. Perhaps happiness is much of a riddle because we usually look for too big an answer. Here, however, we can see how ninety-nine individuals felt happy on their unique days. All of them are witnesses to some of the richest potential in our human lives. They do not embody the world, but they do help us to imagine humanity as a whole. Across our differences, people share a common capability of happiness, and it reminds us of the universal side of our being. Equally, these were all experiences of a particular place and time, since our being is always locally shaped and flavored. *This* is what made someone happy, these pages reveal, on *one* particular day in their life.

Like us, these men and women from the past may have been simply absorbed at the instant they felt good. But soon after, they must have recognized something special about those moments of happiness— and their written records can now pass like sunbeams or a breeze through our own everyday life.

People have, on ordinary days, been glad of life without triumphing over others or accumulating fortunes. Each of these preserved records brings this truth to the fore in a fresh way and with its own shades of meaning.

If human beings seem to become possessed by destructive urges at times, they also have an instinct for the joy of small things. In surprising times and places, the world has appeared like a precious gift.

Public history tends to turn the flow of time into a staccato rhythm of "big" dates: the coronations and resignations, coups and treaties, battles and conquests that supposedly changed the world. By contrast, private history introduces us to "little" days that were important because of what one unique person felt.

As these people from many ways of life wrote down their experiences, there was an inner core that said, "This was a moment when I was happy to be alive." Reading their words now, even centuries later, we can feel immediately how their happiness filled passing moments, creating occasions that needed to be recorded.

Each text, each voice is different, full of a particular life with all its lights and shadows. We are invited by these ninety-nine individuals to share what was specific to their experiences—a place, a time, a relationship. Their ninety-nine moments of joy are arranged by common themes, connected to each other by the natural movement of time from morning to evening.

We gain both wisdom and pleasure from meeting these women and men. We learn naturally about happiness from their stories, which make us happy as well.

These experiences connect with our own lives. Feeling the passion of other people, their zest or deep peace, sudden pleasure or relish for life, their companionship or inwardness, we have new perspectives on the best moments in our own lives.

It is extraordinary how powerful real, remembered happiness is, how deep and true its source. Our happiest lived experiences have the power to help us face the real world with all its difficulties. They exercise a power that the advertised, virtual images and phrases of perfection do not possess. Celebrity and consumption melt away at the merest hint of trouble, but real happiness carries us onward toward the next dawn.

The aim of these pages is to show the enduring value and beauty of ordinary human happiness as we find it in passing moments.

Morning

A Sunday Ride without Worry

Isabella Bird, traveler, writing a letter to her sister

TRUCKEE, CALIFORNIA · AUGUST 31, 1873

This morning Truckee wore a totally different aspect. The crowds of the night before had disappeared. There were heaps of ashes where the fires had been. A sleepy German waiter seemed the only person about the premises, the open drinking saloons were nearly empty, and only a few sleepy-looking loafers hung about in what is called the street. It might have been Sunday; but they say that it [this day] brings a great accession of throng and jollity. Public worship has died out at present; work is discontinued on Sunday, but the day is given up to pleasure. Putting a minimum of indispensables into a bag, and slipping on my Hawaiian riding dress over a silk skirt, and a dust cloak over all, I stealthily crossed the plaza to the livery stable, the largest building in Truckee, where twelve fine horses were stabled in stalls on each side of a broad drive. My friend of the evening before showed me his "rig," three velvet-covered side-saddles almost without horns. Some ladies, he said, used the horn of the Mexican saddle, but none "in the part" rode cavalier fashion [astride]. I felt abashed. I could not ride any distance in the conventional [sidesaddle] mode, and was just going to give up this splendid "ravage," when the man said, "Ride your own fashion; here, at Truckee, if anywhere in the world, people can do as they like." Blissful Truckee! In no time a large grey horse was "rigged out" in a handsome silver-bossed Mexican saddle, with ornamental leather tassels hanging from the stirrup guards, and a housing of black bear's skin. I strapped my silk skirt on the saddle, deposited my cloak in the corn bin, and was safely on the horse's back before his owner had time to devise any way of mounting me. Neither he nor any of the loafers who had assembled showed the slightest sign of astonishment, but all were as respectful as possible.

⁕

Isabella Bird was the daughter of an English vicar. As a child in the 1830s, she had always been ill. Her life seemed to change when she went to America the first time, in 1854, and after that she became an adventurous traveler, whose letters home also made popular books.

3

This morning belongs to a trip to the mountainous West made in 1873, Truckee being near Lake Tahoe and the border between California and Nevada. This was the beginning of her adventure in what had been Gold Rush country, recorded in vividly spontaneous letters to her sister in Scotland.

The railway had only reached this place a few years ago. Surrounded by forests, Truckee was still pioneer country. Here the prospectors had stopped on their way to make their fortunes in California. Bird had arrived the night before to find the town full of bonfires. Around them, the men were drinking, singing, and fighting. She went to her hotel, making her way among the revelers.

Morning seemed to have calmed the place down, leaving only "heaps of ashes." Most of last night's partygoers were still asleep. A few were hanging around listlessly. Businesslike and adventurous, Isabella Bird briskly began her Sunday. With an impartial eye, she noticed that nobody much seemed to be going to church. But apparently she made no judgment. She had come here to get away from the life of a vicar's daughter.

In this sleepy little town, at least on Sunday morning, one place was already awake: the livery stable. Already, the man who ran the stable was up and about. In fact, she had had a word with him as soon as she got to Truckee. Her "friend of the evening before" was expecting her. She cast an expert eye over the horses, appreciating the saddles that he displayed for her inspection.

But then the big question arose. How did ladies ride in this part of the world? This was far more than a practical matter. The man explained, politely, how the women around here generally rode side-saddle rather than "cavalier fashion." It was a moment of dismay for Isabella Bird. She had set her heart on a "ravage," a lovely word for her own private happiness, her outlaw's freedom.

Now she felt uncomfortable, even ashamed, about being different. Perhaps people would laugh at her. The stabler sensed her discomfort and, immediately wanting to put her at ease, told her to ignore what other ladies did and ride the way she chose.

"Blissful Truckee!" Happiness is often found on the other side of the barrier called worry or shame.

Jackdaw Song Breaks the Mist

John James Audubon, ornithologist and artist,
writing in his travel journal

HARDWICK, DERBYSHIRE · OCTOBER 11, 1826

By five o'clock this morning I was running by the Derwent; everything was covered with sparkling congealed dew. The fog arising from the little stream only permitted us to see its waters when they made a ripple against some rock. The vale was all mist, and had I not known where I was, and heard the notes of the Jackdaws above my head, I might have conceived myself walking through a subterraneous passage. But the sun soon began to dispel the mist, and gradually the tops of the trees, the turrets of the castle, and the church pierced through, and stood as if suspended above all objects below. All was calm till a bell struck my ear, when I soon saw the long files of women and little girls moving towards Arkwright's Mills. Almost immediately we started for Bakewell, and breakfasted at the Rutland Arms.

⟜∞⟞

John James Audubon was born in Haiti in 1785 and brought up partly in France. He became a great explorer of the American wilderness, where he had developed his own way of drawing and painting the wildlife, and particularly the birds, of remote and even dangerous places. This is a passage from the journal he kept when he came to crowded Britain, with its busy cities. He was not on vacation. He needed to find subscribers so that he could pay for the publication in book form of his paintings. The security and well-being of his family depended upon this quest, which was ultimately successful and launched his spectacular four-volume *Birds of America*.

Staying in Edinburgh and then Manchester had been a difficult time for a shy man who loved open spaces. But this morning was better. Small pleasures joined together to yield a moment of special happiness, perhaps when he least expected it.

First, there was his simple pleasure in running free by the River Derwent after many days spent in cramped and uncongenial cities. Early morning let him be alone at last, something he was used to. Mist covered everything, turning the world new, making a real beginning to more than just another day. There is something about the phrase "sparkling congealed dew" that captures the way this sight was a tactile pleasure. It was as if the early light were sticking to all surfaces, and yet there can be nothing smoother than something that sparkles.

The fog played over the waters, creating miniature images of water and stone, "a ripple against some rock." In Audubon's words, these impressions are curiously sudden and real. The small ripples seem to emerge into existence as if out of some original chaos. They are tiny acts of creation.

In a foreign country, and a misty vale, he felt strange, as if this place was nowhere on earth—"a subterraneous passage." But one sound proved that the world was still there. Birdsong! Audubon had spent so much of his life watching birds in America. For him, this was the first sound in the world, and the best, too. And he recognized the species —jackdaws. This, too, was part of his happiness. He was in a strange country, but the things he loved were there as well. That was all he needed.

Through the misty haziness, little fragments of his surroundings appeared, "the tops of the trees, the turrets of the castle." Objects are far more poignant when they materialize this way. Seemingly weightless, they hang in the air, free of all the usual downward pressures, just as Audubon himself must have felt free on that autumn morning.

Buoyed up, he went back to his search for financial support with renewed vigor. It was the song of jackdaws that told him on that morning he was fully alive. His glorious paintings have done the same for countless viewers.

A Plunge into Cold Water

Friedrich Schleiermacher, philosopher, writing a letter to his sister

BERLIN · AUGUST 13, 1797

Carl [Schleiermacher's younger brother] and I have conceived the idea, which has been approved by the doctors, that it would be very good for us both, but more especially for me, to bathe frequently. Now, as there is a very well-arranged bathing-house at about a hundred paces from my lodgings, Carl comes several times a week at five or six o'clock in the morning to fetch me. Of course, he finds me still in bed, and with me that means the same as asleep; and what a pleasurable awaking it is, when I hear his footsteps in the passage, and he comes in so full of friendliness and bids me good morning. In the greatest hurry I then don my clothes; in the meantime he fills a pipe, and then we start. In a safe bathing-room we lave our limbs in the somewhat coldish waters of the Planke, a little tributary of the Spree [a river running through Berlin]; at first shuddering at the cold, then laughing at our own cowardice; and, after the plunge, feeling extremely well and cheerful. On our return, Carl breakfasts with me, generally on milk, or, on festive occasions, on chocolate; and while this is being partaken of, we chat, or read, or perhaps play a game at chess, and then each to his work. As Carl cannot begin his occupations in the laboratory before seven, he does not neglect any duty in consequence of this bathing, and it has procured to us many a happy hour which we should not otherwise have enjoyed.

Today we have again had one of our bathing mornings, and subsequently we graced our breakfast by sensible reading of a chemical work.

Friedrich Schleiermacher was a hospital chaplain in Berlin when he wrote this letter to his sister, Charlotte, with whom he maintained an open and extremely personal correspondence. In his late twenties, he was beginning to participate in the intellectual life of the city. There was a new emphasis on individual experience and imagination that he was coming to share, as he emerged from many years of private doubt and melancholy. He would soon be the leading figure in

European religious thought, but in 1797 he was still making his way.

Here he is telling their sister about his visits from his younger brother, Carl, who was pursuing the new science of chemistry at a laboratory in Berlin. They have decided to go bathing several mornings a week. He explains that this is "approved by the doctors," perhaps because it might otherwise be seen as frivolous. The family tradition was puritanical.

In his theology, Schleiermacher would later emphasize, against the strict tradition he grew up in, that human beings are made of both body and spirit and that the physical dimension cannot be dismissed as merely an obstacle to salvation. In this letter, he talks of a "pleasurable awaking" that feels like both a spiritual and a bodily pleasure.

As he got dressed, he could smell the scent of his brother's pipe tobacco. It was the beginning of an experience that engaged all his senses. Together, they went to the appointed and safe bathing place, where they plunged into the "somewhat coldish waters," leaving them "shuddering." Then the shudder turned to laughter and the gusto of being fully alive in this world for another day.

They returned home "feeling extremely well and cheerful," healthy in both body and mind. The breakfast was also special. The brothers enjoyed little harmless pleasures, a touch of self-indulgence. Milk ordinarily, yes, but sometimes even chocolate! (Hot chocolate was perfect after the cold dip.) The chemical book was part of this pleasure, since knowledge was also something to be appreciated.

Two years later, Schleiermacher preached an Easter sermon to the king of Prussia, in which he imagined the end of life: "But the last heartbeat is not really the end of life; life ceases with the last thought and feeling that our spirit brings forth in union with its body." Those mornings spent with his brother had given him a deep sense of renewal; each morning had been a chance to plunge afresh into life itself.

The First Glow of Sun on the Wet Mountain

Hsu Hsia-k'o, gentleman traveler,
starting his travel journal

T'IEN-T'AI SHAN, CHINA · MAY 13, 1613

Rained in the morning, but we set off. A ride brought us to a fork in the road. The mountains being steep and the road slippery, we alighted from our horses and walked. Now after some bends we were up on a ridge, and here the sunshine lit up the wet mountain.

∽∞∾

Hsu Hsia-k'o was from a well-off family and he was a scholar. At thirty-one, this was his first trip into such remote territory as this sparsely peopled, mountainous region, a land of monasteries and holy places. Some Buddhist monasteries, founded as early as the middle of the third century CE, were close by.

Taking with him some servants and a friend who was a monk, Hsu set off into the rainy morning. This was the first day of their adventure, a damp spring morning in China. Unfamiliar mountains rose high into the sky around him. Here the Taoists, whom he admired, found the fundamental elements of existence: earth, water, and sky.

Yesterday had been a bright and cloudless day. But today it was dreary, and there were even rumors of tigers in this part of the world. It was alarming to think of these great cats being nearby, and they were even reported to have killed people during the past month. Altogether it could have been an anxious and unsettling morning, but the travelers set off resolutely.

Through the rain, they advanced up the slope. At first, they rode on horseback. But soon, they had to dismount and walk. Gradually, the weather changed. The way curved from side to side up the mountain. At last the gradient eased off and they had reached the ridge. With perfect synchronicity, the sun came out.

Suddenly, the mountainside glittered from all the water. The discomfort of journeying through the rain had turned into magic on that first morning of Hsu's new life. The mundane had become sublime. Difficulty had turned into a blessing. Round one corner, he had arrived instantaneously in a different world.

Here on a suddenly bright day, a man just past his youth had seen the clean, sharp outline of everything. He was on his way to the first summit. The whole day opened up beautifully after that first glitter of sunlight: "Gurgling springs and dewy hills. The azaleas too were aflame on the green hillsides."

Until then, Hsu Hsia-k'o had had no clear goals or precise ambitions. Pursuing this journey and then others, he became one of the great travelers and travel writers in Chinese history. This first moment of happiness as he rounded the last bend on the slippery mountain road was enough to send him on his way in life itself.

Keen Air on Christmas Day

Henry White, clergyman and amateur scientist, writing in his diary

FYFIELD, HAMPSHIRE · CHRISTMAS DAY, 1784

Christmas Day, very bright morn. Trees beautifully powdered with rime [icy frost], more severity of freezing than any since the very first beginning, very little wind but the air amazingly keen. Sound of bells heard from all the villages on every side. Service at Fyfield. Riding not unpleasant over the open fields and downs. Trees powdered most amazingly by the rime, make a very picturesque appearance at Tidworth.

❧

In 1784, Henry White, a middle-aged vicar in the small English village of Fyfield, noticed that something was wrong with the weather. From the middle of summer, there was a thick, poisonous-smelling fog. The autumn was also strange. Not only did the fog persist but the temperatures fell lower than he could remember, and he had been recording them for many years.

Christmas Eve had ended with the unsettling return of this weird fog, as he had recorded sitting in his vicarage: "Thermometer at sunset down to 20 [Fahrenheit], very thick rimy, stinking fog came on after sunset. Very bitter, fierce frost again tonight. The thermometer registered 10 [Fahrenheit]."

By "rimy," White meant cold and icy. He had gotten used to talking about this "rimy, stinking fog" as he noted the strangeness of the December cold in his diary. He was too scientific to feel superstitious about this mysterious fog, but it was clearly associated with the bitterness of the nights.

In fact, he was recording a Europe-wide event, the cloud of sulfurous smoke that followed a huge volcanic eruption in Iceland that occurred in 1783/84. It caused many deaths across Europe, and the several years of bad harvests that followed may even have contributed to the unrest that led to the French Revolution in 1789. This intruding fog was indeed a widespread threat, making its presence felt in the English countryside on Christmas Eve.

Henry White and his wife, Elizabeth, had lived at the vicarage for more than twenty years. Their eldest son was at university, their youngest child was five. They were busy with family life and local duties, caring for the poor of the parish. But this stinking fog seemed to have come into their world like a malevolent external power.

But now, as he looked outside on Christmas morning, something was different. He temporarily omitted to record the precise temperature. No longer the amateur scientist, he was awake to something special in the air. The wind had calmed down. The air was "amazingly keen." It was as if the world was insisting that he notice it. And also that he notice his own presence.

A sense of perfection returned several times during this day: the sounds of the bells clear in the air, the shape of the trees outlined, yet also softened, by the frost. That foggy rime ceased to be uncanny and became instead a kind of gleaming beauty, overlaying the familiar details of Henry White's surroundings. It was impossible to see the trees and hedges without wanting to touch them, to feel this powdery, frosty quality instead of the usual unyielding surfaces.

This keen morning brought before all the senses the sheer wonder of creation. The fog was dispelled and even the temperature rose back to a more seasonal thirty degrees Fahrenheit on the afternoon of this English Christmas Day.

A Glorious Sunrise Dispels the Gloom

Patrick Kenny, priest, writing in his diary

NEW CASTLE, DELAWARE · MAY 9, 1826

This morning, about 1 hour and ½ before sunrise, offered to the eye the grandest exhibition of divine power blazing forth from the E. by N. in the inexpressible golden tinge on the sky from N.E. to S.E. The nearer the vast Luminary approached, the more the eastern horizon seemed to dart, or pour forward a sea of fire, whose waves were met by a cloud from the west, as extensive and as gloomy, as the eastern panorama was vivid and enchanting. Just as the sun's disk danced on the summit of our neighbouring hills, the black cloud dissolved in a smart and long continued rain; this latter proves to be a blessing to the parched fields, for it did not stop our corn works.

⁗

Patrick Kenny had arrived in Wilmington, Delaware, in the summer of 1804. Born in Dublin in 1763, he had come to America to serve as a missionary and priest to the small Catholic congregations in this area. The heat affected him so badly that he tried immediately to return to Ireland, but all the places for the voyage back were taken. Reluctantly, he stayed and soon was ministering to a congregation in West Chester, Pennsylvania. He also visited regularly a number of smaller "stations." In 1805, he moved to a farm at White Clay Creek, New Castle, Delaware, belonging to the Jesuit order. There he stayed until his death in 1840. He renamed the farm "Coffee Run," and it was from one of its windows that he appreciated this May sunrise.

His diary is full of sympathy, humor, but also grumbling, often about the pain from a sore leg. In April 1826, he was in his early sixties, and he often felt he was getting too old, especially for the long journeys he had to make to outlying congregations and individuals. He knew everyone's troubles, from lost cows to family illness.

Patrick Kenny had not gotten up early this May morning for the sake of it. There was too much to do for lying in. Still, when he looked outside the window, he forgot for a moment why he was awake at this early hour. He had a long day ahead of him, with farmwork and

13

required visits, but now he just watched the sun gradually rise, as if it were being painted right before his eyes.

His record begins scholarly and precise, the sun rising not just in the east but from northeast to southeast. He knows exactly how long it is going to take for the whole sky to light up, because he is used to this time of the night. The "golden tinge" of light is the bare minimum of morning. Though his language is at times grand and conventional—"Luminary" and such like words—there is something very personal about this love for the very first light; it is never more distinct from darkness than at this borderline moment.

His own language seems to catch energy from the rising sun: "a sea of fire," "the sun's disk danced on the summit." He loves the conflict between fire and water as the sunshine and the rain cloud are contending for possession of this new day. It would have been easy to moralize and think of good and evil, but he resists the temptation.

He must have stood still for an hour or more to see the sun dance along the hills. It is this stillness of the watcher that complements the drama of the scene in the sky. He never states his happiness; it is simply there in his steady attention.

At last the rain begins to fall. It is like the release of confined pressure as "the black cloud dissolved in a smart and long continued rain."

Soon Patrick Kenny was back to the everyday troubles of his long workweek: "Called yesterday evening by Mrs. John Fox of Wilmington to visit her; this day she is taken ill with pleurisy. A most inconvenient call, in my most inconvenient week. Last Sunday's journey to Brandywine, this day's to Wilmington, next Friday's to Wilmington again, and Friday afternoon's to Newcastle, and Saturday's to Wilmington for church on Sunday, and Monday's to Philadelphia, and on my return, my journey to West Chester and home. If I shall be able to hobble thro', God alone can give." But that hour at dawn must have remained as a weeklong beacon of inspiration to him.

The Urge to Linger in a Warm Bed

Marcus Aurelius, Roman emperor,
writing in his book of reflections

WITH THE ROMAN LEGIONS IN CENTRAL EUROPE · BETWEEN 170 AND 180 CE

When you are drowsy in a morning, and find a reluctance to getting out of your bed, make this reflection with yourself: "I must rise to discharge the duties incumbent on me as a man. And shall I do with reluctance what I was born to do, and what I came into the world to do? What! Was I formed for no other purpose than to lie sunk in down, and indulge myself in a warm bed?"— "But a warm bed is comfortable and pleasant," you will say.—Were you born then only to please yourself; and not for action, and the exertion of your faculties? Do not you see the very shrubs, the sparrows, the ants, the spiders, and the bees, all busied, and in their several stations co-operating to adorn the system of the universe?

And do you alone refuse to discharge the duties of man, instead of performing with alacrity the part allotted you by nature? "But some rest and relaxation," you will urge, "is necessary."—Very true; yet nature has prescribed bounds to this indulgence, as she also has to our eating and drinking. But you exceed the bounds of moderation, and what is sufficient, in this instance. Though I must confess, where business is concerned, you consult your ease, and keep within moderate limits.

⸎

Marcus Aurelius became the Roman emperor in 161 CE, when he was forty years old. By the time he wrote these thoughts—in Greek—in his book of philosophical reflections, he had been one of the most powerful men on earth for over a decade. His empire stretched from North Africa to England and from Syria to Spain. For a while, he had shared responsibility with his brother—now he ruled alone. During the decade before his death in 180 CE, he spent much time on military campaigns in Central Europe. Everywhere he went, he took his writing.

Now, eighteen hundred years later, the empire is long gone. Highways and train tracks run where straight roads took his legions. But the words that he wrote down, presumably morning and night, live on.

Marcus Aurelius is famous as a stoic philosopher, a thinker whose ideas are stern and morally demanding. As human beings, we have a duty, whether emperor or citizen, to give our best.

Nothing was too small for the emperor to offer advice on it. Here he imagined he was talking to somebody who was just waking up in the morning. As befitted both a stoic and a commander, his advice was to rise and greet the day. There was work to be done. He must have had that thought on many days as the sun rose over the war-torn land. Yet as we listen to this stern and serious voice, we can hear something all too human within it: here is a man who knows that there is nothing more pleasurable "than to lie sunk in down, and indulge myself in a warm bed." There is such a strong sensation of the comfort and warmth inside the bed, a refuge from all the difficulties that await. He is said to have had trouble going to sleep, and if so, this drowsy time in the morning would have been even more restful, bringing the long-awaited ease.

He knew, like us, that he had to get up; and he felt all the more the pleasure of lingering in what was perhaps the softest bed in the Roman Empire. This contented self even replied to the moralist that for all the moral imperatives of duty, "a warm bed is comfortable and pleasant."

Soon enough, of course, he countered with arguments and logic. Across much of Europe and northern Africa and out to the East he ruled his empire, even though there were continuous revolts. Not many people have been more powerful in the history of the world than Marcus Aurelius. But the reason we still care about his words is that he knew about simple pleasures, too.

The disproportion between the description of the warm bed and the vast military empire outside is touching. It reveals something important about the true sources of happiness, before the stoic emperor is obliged to move on.

Winter Dawn in the Cathedral Close

Anna Seward, writer, composing a poem

LICHFIELD, STAFFORDSHIRE · DECEMBER 19, 1782

I love to rise ere gleams the tardy light,
Winter's pale dawn; and as warm fires illume,
And cheerful tapers shine around the room,
Thro' misty windows bend my musing sight
Where, round the dusky lawn, the mansions white,
With shutters clos'd, peer faintly thro' the gloom,
That slow recedes; while yon grey spires assume,
Rising from their dark pile, an added height
By indistinctness given. Then to decree
The grateful thoughts to God, ere they unfold
To Friendship, or the Muse, or seek with glee
Wisdom's rich page: O, hours! more worth than gold,
By whose blest use we lengthen life, and free
From drear decays of age, outlive the old!

❧

Anna Seward was the daughter of an eminent clergyman. He became senior canon of Lichfield Cathedral in the English Midlands in 1750, when she was eight years old. They were given the Bishop's Palace in the cathedral close, since the bishop did not want it, and the senior canon was next in rank. These poetic lines were written in the bedroom where Anna Seward had begun most days since that time, thirty-two years before. Even now, as a middle-aged woman, the associations and memories were strong. She had never married, despite some romances. She had, though, become a well-respected poet and friend of such famous writers as Samuel Johnson.

She awoke on that December morning just before dawn. Christmas was not far away. She felt anew the sensation of another day unfolding. "I love to rise" describes this moment, and also many others that she remembered with pleasure. The fire was warming in the grate, now as always. The candles were lit around the room, and it seems as

17

if both she and these "tapers" shared in the "cheerful" feeling. The windowpanes were "misty" with cold. Then she peered outside.

The outlines of the buildings in the close, "mansions white," were just emerging from the dark. Further off, the three spires of the cathedral were starting to materialize, more impressive for their "indistinctness" than when clear daylight revealed their proportions. Of course, she knew every detail of this scene. Yet the mystery never passed. This was a moment when the close hovered between absence and presence, shadow and solidity. This was a moment she loved, so full of possibilities each dawn.

Like other poets of her time, Anna Seward was inclined to draw general lessons and give advice. It was particularly tempting for a woman who was developing a literary reputation to prove that she was as serious a writer as the men. This poem is a sonnet, one of the most difficult forms of Western poetry. It divides in the middle of the ninth line, and the latter part is certainly moral and religious.

But the beginning is different.

There was no greater happiness for Anna Seward than this moment of opposites—warmth and cold, inside and outside, waking and dreaming. This December morning, the world once again kept its covenant with her, as it does for all people on good days.

Friendship

Time Together with an Ancient Book

Willem de Clercq, student, writing in his journal

AMSTERDAM · 1813

Last Tuesday I began to read with Crommelin the second book of Virgil. I declare that this reading greatly pleased me. We made good progress, without getting too far or perfectly understanding what we were reading; but how beautiful this Virgil is and what a pleasure in one's life to get to know such great authors.

This Crommelin is one of my very oldest friends whom I have been very happy to rediscover. He has been wandering for a long time in foreign towns and he returned at last to his hometown. He has acquired lots of knowledge and is also a very passionate friend of literature.

⁓∞⁓

In 1813, Willem was eighteen years old, living in his father's home in Amsterdam. They were well-off people, though not extravagantly wealthy. All around, there was the excitement and clamor of Napoleonic Europe: the French emperor held power in the Low Countries at the time. His invasion of Russia had failed, but there was still the last energy of the regime in the air. Willem had just begun to keep a journal, which in fact accompanied him through the rest of his life. Most of it was to be in Dutch, but during these early years he wrote in French.

He was an energetic person, serious and focused. Later on, he became a leading poet, a religious thinker, and also a founder of the Dutch textiles industry. Here, though, he recorded an ordinary Tuesday when two young men sat down together and opened a large volume with text in Latin. It was one of the works that Willem knew were considered the classics of the European past.

Perhaps because of the contemporary French Empire, he turned to the story of the legendary founding of the original European empire, ancient Rome. Virgil's first-century BCE epic poem described the story of Aeneas, as he made his way from defeated Troy to the site of the future city of empire.

Willem's friend was about the same age but he had more experience of the world. Crommelin had been "for a long time in foreign
towns." They had lost touch during those years. Now, Willem was
glad to pick up the threads of their old friendship. He was impressed
by how much his friend knew about life. Above all, though, he was
happy because they shared the same passion for reading. As they sat
together, turning the pages and struggling to understand the Latin
sentences, they were kept going by this shared intensity. It was a day
of real communion together.

Their Latin was perhaps a little weak. They were not able to understand everything perfectly, but they kept on going as best they could.
This was not a mechanical exercise in translation. Even though they
did not grasp everything perfectly, they made out enough to realize
"how beautiful this Virgil is" and to have a genuine experience of
literature—"what a pleasure in one's life to get to know such great
authors."

This was really a threefold moment of friendship, since the two
young men were joined in spirit by a third companion, the poet Virgil
himself. It was almost as if he was there with them. The friends felt
that they had entered into the select company of ancient European
civilization.

There was also time to chat about their lives. Willem was eager to
learn about his friend's travels—and became upset when he heard
how restrictive Crommelin's father had been: "His father, though, is
a bigoted man. He never allowed his son to go to see a play or to have
a game of cards. What ridiculous childishness!"

All of it together made up this moment of friendship: the ancient
story, the associations with their school days, and the gossip about
their lives. While outside Napoleonic Europe entered its last years,
two young men had a happy Tuesday together.

A Climb to the Top of the Hill

Kamo no Chomei, poet and former courtier,
composing a short memoir

THE FOOTHILLS OF MOUNT HINO, JAPAN · 1212

At the foot of the hill stands a wooden hut, which is where the hill's care-taker resides. With him lives a young child [the caretaker's son] who sometimes comes to visit me. When he has nothing else to do, he joins me for a stroll. He is sixteen and I am sixty; but although our ages are far apart, we take pleasure in the same things. Sometimes we pick grass and berries, or gather yams and parsley. Other times, we go down to the rice paddies at the foot of the hill, and make sheaves of the leftover ears.

On fine days we climb up to the peak; gazing at the distant sky over my old home, we see Mt. Kohata, Fushimi village, Toba and Hatsukashi. Nobody owns this view, and nothing will stop us from enjoying it [. . .] Depending on the season, on the way home we gather cherry blossoms, or look for maple leaves, or snap off bracken, or pick fruit and nuts; some of these I offer to the Buddha, and some I take home with me.

⌘

In 1212, when he wrote this passage, Kamo no Chomei was living alone in a small hut that he had built in the mountains. He had been a successful poet at the Japanese court, but eight years ago, he had taken Buddhist vows and given up court life, retiring to his secluded home.

This text is from a work called *Hojo-ki* (*The Ten-Foot-Square Hut*). Other passages give more detail of that hut and the setting. For example, there were luxuriant clumps of bracken fern growing along the east side of the hut, while to the north there was a little garden with a modest fence of brushwood. The hut merged with the natural world.

Everything was carefully arranged in Kamo no Chomei's solitary home. There was a small shrine, placed so that it caught the light of the setting sun. He had boxes of poetry books and the music of nature in the background, a harp, and a writing desk by the window. It was all neat—and could have been lonely.

But he was friendly with the man who looked after the hillside. Such an easygoing relationship between different social ranks was possible only outside the finely tuned society of court and capital. Here people of every rank talked to each other.

Even more surprising, as he acknowledged, was his companionship with the caretaker's son: "He is sixteen and I am sixty; but although our ages are far apart, we take pleasure in the same things." It was the most spontaneous friendship, founded on a natural convergence of tastes and inclinations. This was different from all the rigid distinctions with which he had lived at court.

Together, former courtier and young peasant wandered the countryside and shared simple pleasures. As equals, they roamed the fields or searched for berries, nuts, and other little things.

There were many happy moments together. The finest was when they climbed "up to the peak" and the old man looked out across the land. From this vantage point, next to his friend, he saw the places where he had lived—and once been important: "Gazing at the distant sky over my old home, we see Mt. Kohata, Fushimi village, Toba and Hatsukashi." He had turned down a request by the emperor that he should return to his post among the poets. He did not want to be back down there among the wealthy and the powerful, the ambitious and the proud.

Up here, the view was free in every sense. He was able to enjoy the moment—with his young friend, but without needing permission from anyone.

A Breakfast Served with
Stories and Laughter

George Cutler, law student, writing in his diary

LITCHFIELD, CONNECTICUT · NOVEMBER 29, 1820

For the moon was bright, the snow full of reflection, I full of breakfast, and Nate [his horse] full of fire; while the cocks of the country crowed about us for music and the stars shot this way and that about the heavens, as if making a display of fireworks for our amusement. All was silent. As we rose [rode up] the hills and looked back upon the far distance which ran down the valley to the southeast, the two extremes of the splendour of the united powers of snow and moonbeams and the contrasted darkness of the deep ravines into which light would not penetrate, filled the whole view. I often stopped to admire the cold but burnished beauties of the prospect and felt the magnificence of the scene.

I found George up, though I little expected it when I turned a corner to take a look at his window. I had little thought of seeing a light there at that time of the night—I ran upstairs, opened the door an inch and inquired if Mr. Gibbs lived there. Then we laughed ourselves to death and disturbed the neighbours. Mr. Chambers in the backroom inquired who the Devil had come, and being told, said, he "thought t'was him."

Breakfasted there and told stories till I thought I had told too many [. . .]

When I turned my face homeward I felt the inconvenience of 3 pairs of pantaloons, 2 of stockings, 2 shirts and 2 great coats.

Now I think my ride too good a one to grumble about.

◦≫◦

George Cutler had come to the town of Litchfield in Connecticut to study law with Judge Tapping Reeve, after graduating from Yale University in 1816. This was the first formal law school course in the country, and Cutler was admitted fully to the American Bar in 1821. Meanwhile, he had a number of friends taking the same course. There was a girls' academy nearby, too, and so Litchfield was full of young people like Cutler and his friend and fellow student George Gibbs, with whom he shared this fine breakfast recorded on a cold November morning.

George Cutler loved Litchfield. He liked the people and the setting, as another entry (of the same year) in his diary shows: "Aug. 18 (Evening). Miss Talmadge here is certainly elegant; there is no such woman in New Haven. Litchfield is certainly an extraordinary place for beauty. The mountain air gives them the expression of health." At the end of September, he had taken the oath as an attorney. It was a successful time.

This very early morning at the end of November gave him the special moment to seal his happiness. He was already in a good mood when he set off, having had an early breakfast, with his horse equally lively. He felt as if nature was staging a grand performance for him, with shooting stars and moonbeams and music from the crowing cocks.

But he became even happier when he met his friend. He arrived at the lodging house where George Gibbs resided, and to his surprise saw a light in Gibbs's room. Eagerly, he "ran upstairs" and, jokingly, asked formally for "Mr. Gibbs." Then their peals of laughter rang out loud in the silence. It was a wonderful feeling. They also had the pleasure of annoying the man in the backroom.

It was as if they owned this dawn. George Cutler had his second breakfast, full of gossip and chatter this time.

What made this moment so unique was the contrast with the solemn "magnificence" of the night on his way there. It made him appreciate the warmth of human friendship, having just experienced alone the overwhelming expanse of the universe. Here, at the lodging house, breakfast was a happy time for friends together.

The Freedom of Dancing
through the Night

Robert Burns, poet and farmer,
writing a letter to a friend

SCOTTISH HIGHLANDS · JUNE 30, 1787

On our return, at a Highland gentleman's hospitable mansion, we fell in with a merry party, and danced till the ladies left us, at three in the morning. Our dancing was none of the French or English insipid formal movements; the ladies sung Scotch songs like angels, at intervals; then we flew at the Bab at the bowster, Tullochgorum and Loch Erroch side [Highland dances], etc. like midges sporting in the sun, or craws [crows] prognosticating a storm [. . .] When the dear lasses left us, we ranged round the bowl till good-fellow hour of six; except a few minutes that we went out to pay our devotions to the glorious lamp of day peering over the towering top of Benlomond [mountain]. We all kneeled; our worthy landlord's son held the bowl; each man a full glass in his hand; and I, as priest, repeated some rhyming nonsense, like Thomas a Rhymer's prophecies.

❦

Robert Burns, now regarded as the national poet of Scotland, was twenty-eight when he wrote this letter to his friend James Smith about a summer night in the wild Scottish Highlands. Burns had published his first book of poems, which instantly turned him from a struggling farmer into a literary celebrity. Now he was escaping from Edinburgh, where he had been feted, into the countryside.

Burns loved his summer trip in the Highlands, which he described in another letter to his friend as "a country where savage streams tumble over savage mountains, thinly overspread with savage flocks." This June 30 was the best night of a wonderful summer of freedom.

There were two great social pleasures that night. First, there was the company that was dancing together, men and women, until three in the morning: "the ladies sung Scotch songs like angels, at intervals; then we flew at the Bab at the bowster, Tullochgorum and Loch Erroch side." These were fiddle tunes that he could play himself.

They had danced the popular dances. They knew these rhythms, because they had grown up with them. These were the songs and tunes of a rural way of life, and he was happy that the members of the party could share this music together.

At the height of the enjoyment, Burns suddenly had a vision as if from far away. He seemed to see them all, moving like tiny insects in the air, "like midges sporting in the sun."

The vision only amused him, and now another, perhaps even greater, pleasure followed the dancing. After the women had gone to bed, the men carried on drinking until six in the morning. Noticing the light in the sky, they went outside and welcomed the dawn together. They all kneeled, with the landlord's son holding the ceremonial bowl and Burns "as priest" chanting some crazy rhymes to greet the new day. It was fun but also held a deeper happiness. He experienced an absolute joy at being alive, alive together with friends in the Highlands to see a new "day peering over the towering top of Benlomond."

Later in the same letter he confessed to being still unsure of his path in the world, since he had "yet fixed on nothing with respect to the serious business of life. I am, just as usual, a rhyming, mason-making, raking, aimless, idle fellow." Doubts lurked in his mind about whether he really wanted the life that his literary success was bringing him.

But on this night, he had been briefly free of those nagging doubts. It was the company of friends that had freed him from his inner struggles.

In Anticipation of a Gentleman's Visit

Mary Russell Mitford, writer, composing a letter to a friend

READING, BERKSHIRE · APRIL 5, 1814

I think you must have guessed, my dear Sir William [Elford], when I talked of presumptuous hopes, or rather presumptuous wishes (I don't think I got so far as hopes), that I was impudent enough to desire [. . .] that you would favour us with a visit here [. . .]

I suspect, however, that you have as much pleasure in pleasing as in being pleased—in making happy as in being happy; that in default of greenhouse plants (and our greenhouse is a real vegetable churchyard—a collection of dead stumps and withered leaves), you will be well content with cowslips and wood anemones; and instead of beaux and belles, will graciously accept the company of a whole flight of nightingales whom I have invited to meet you. And, in conclusion, that unless it is absolutely inconvenient (and, unreasonable as you may think me, I am not unreasonable enough even to wish you to come if it is), you will give your poor little fat friend the happiness of seeing you.

⁓∞⁓

Mary Mitford lived with her parents just outside the English town of Reading. They had a grand house that her father, a doctor, had built. But he had only been enabled to do so by the proceeds of a winning lottery ticket that Mary had chosen at the age of ten. An extravagant gambler from an aristocratic background, his losses were on the way to ruining the family despite this good fortune, as he had done before— that was why she was looking round at the ramshackle greenhouse.

Mary Mitford was a resilient woman. In her late twenties, she was already a recognized poet and, some years later, would also become an extremely successful novelist, maintaining her parents when all else had failed. Sir William Elford, her correspondent, was a gentleman artist with whom she had become friendly. Their correspondence was regular and detailed. He was married, with two children, and his friendship with Mitford was a close one, without romantic undertones on either side.

The opening paragraph in this letter expressed her modest hope that he might come to visit, since she was unable to travel at that time to see him in Bath. Her letter was full of the sound of her voice, as if she was talking in person. She talked, especially, about happiness, playing with the theme when she elegantly complimented Sir William on his taste for giving pleasure to others. In other words, he would be glad to cheer her up, even if it was no great treat for him. It was a beautifully modulated plea for his company. It also suggested that she already began to feel happy even in imagining his arrival at her rather somber home. She signed herself with a modest smile as his "little fat friend," "fat" being a way she sometimes referred to herself that was wryly relaxed.

Her humor started to light up the world around her, turning the ruined greenhouse into "a real vegetable churchyard," a sight worth seeing. She seemed to become happier about her home and her life, as she began to see them through the eyes of a visiting friend. The greenhouse was derelict, but instead there was the natural beauty of "cowslips and wood anemones." It was not the society world of Bath, with all the "beaux and belles" like in a Jane Austen ballroom; she could conjure up "a whole flight of nightingales" instead. That was the "company" she imagined inviting to welcome her visitor.

The nightingales were already singing in Mary Mitford's thoughts as she wrote the letter. It would be another moment of happiness when he arrived, but she was happy enough already just thinking of it for now.

The Familiar Delight of Chitchat

Sarah Connell, schoolgirl, writing in her diary

ANDOVER, MASSACHUSETTS · JANUARY 10, 1808

Saturday 9th [. . .] In the afternoon Papa and myself set off in a sleigh for Ando-
ver [. . .] We stopped some time at Hill's tavern, and arrived at Aunt Osgood's
[in Andover] at about five o'clock. Received a friendly welcome from Harriot
and her Mama [Mrs. Osgood]. [. . .] I had so much to hear, and say, that I did
not retire till late.

Sunday 10th. There was no meeting [Quaker assembly] here all day [. . .]
In the evening [. . .] Papa, Harriot and myself went over to Doctor Kittredge's.
Papa promised to meet them in Gloucester on the Wednesday following. Had
a long and friendly chit-chat with Harriot. We sat around the blazing hearth,
sweet sociability prevails, and cheerfulness smiles throughout our little circle.
May the angel of domestic peace hover over our dwelling.

Sarah was sixteen when she wrote this cheerful record of a return
visit. She was going to see friends with whom she had gone to school
at Andover, until she had returned home to her family in Newburyport, Massachusetts, six months before. She went with her father,
George Connell, a sea captain and merchant, and was happiest of
all to see Harriot Osgood, her cousin and best friend, with whom
she had shared a room at the Osgood home during the school year.
The Kittredges had a large, hospitable house nearby, where Sarah
had also spent many good days; Maria Kittredge was another close
school friend.

When Sarah had moved back to Newburyport, it had been one of
the saddest moments of her young life: "Painful indeed were my sensations on leaving Aunt Osgood's happy dwelling, and the moment
that separated me from friends so tenderly beloved will never be
obliterated from my mind." She had known she would miss Harriot:
"I felt a reluctance to bid farewell to that literary institution, of which
I had long been a member. My busy imagination pictured my beloved
Harriot and myself, walking cheerfully to the Academy, our books in

our hands, anxious only to recite well. But no longer shall we tread together the path of literature."

Until six months ago, she and Harriot had spent most of each day together, and they had talked for long evenings about everything. Now that she had come for a visit, the old ease was still there. The two young women picked up where they had left off: "Papa, Harriot and myself went over to Doctor Kittredge's." At last, she could have "a long and friendly chit-chat with Harriot."

There was no strangeness between them. They had not, as she might have feared, grown apart. It was just perfect "chit-chat," the most relaxed thing in the world—companionship that was slow and easy, never in a rush to be done and gone. Simply being together was the point of this special occasion.

Sarah was aware why she felt so good. It was because here, "sweet sociability prevails, and cheerfulness smiles." This was real human contact, with the added comfort of a fire crackling in the background. There is something quite philosophical about this moment, when a young person realizes that one secret of her happiness is something within reach, almost too common to be noticed.

A Casual Dinner Party

Horace, poet and philosopher, writing to a friend

OUTSIDE ROME · SEPTEMBER 22, CA. 20 BCE

If you can sit upon a paltry seat,
My friend Torquatus, and endure to eat
A homely dish, a salad all the treat:
Sir, I shall make a feast, my friends invite,
And beg that you wou'd sup with me tonight.
My liquor flow'd from the Minturnian vine,
In Taurus' Consulship, 'tis common wine;
If you have better, let your flasks be sent;
Or let what I, the lord, provide, content.
My servants sweep and furnish ev'ry room,
My dishes all are cleans'd against you come:
Forbear thy wanton hopes, and toil for gain,
And Moschus' cause; 'tis all but idle pain.
Tomorrow Caesar's Birthday comes, to give
Release to cares, and a small time to live.
Then we may sleep 'till Noon, and gay delight
And merry talk prolong the summer's night.

⁂

Two thousand years ago, the poet Horace wrote this letter in verse, inviting his friend Manlius Torquatus, a distinguished lawyer, to a leisurely dinner party at his farm outside Rome. Horace was a man in middle age, a famous poet, whose patron, Maecenas, was a close advisor to the emperor Augustus (Caesar in this poem). The origins of Horace were far from grand, his father having been a slave who purchased his freedom and provided for his son's education, which laid the foundation of his career as a writer. The farm was a gift from Maecenas (whose name has become synonymous with patronage of the arts) in recognition of several volumes of poetry that were highly regarded at court.

Torquatus was a Roman aristocrat, as were the other guests that evening. Horace invited him to come and sit "upon a paltry seat." The occasion would still be exclusive and carefully arranged, but not as grand as their usual banquets. The wine would be "common," no luxury vintage. "Minturnian" was a brand of everyday Roman wine, harvested about six years earlier, when Taurus was consul. If he wanted better, Torquatus would have to bring his own.

Horace was preparing, in his own way, to have his idea of a perfect night. Though simple, everything would be clean and neat. The food (salad!) would not be fancy but tasty and well-presented. It would be a truly hospitable get-together.

The occasion was to celebrate the birthday of Augustus. The next day was a Roman holiday, so there would be no work to make them get up. Leave your usual business, the poet advised his friend, in the law courts and high finance (Torquatus had defended a man named Moschus against a charge of poisoning)—now seize the moment of conviviality.

Then he drew a picture of real happiness. Since they could sleep in the next morning, this night would give "release to cares," freedom from the usual concerns. They could stay up and chat ("merry talk") into the small hours. For Horace, being able to invite his friends to such an occasion was already giving him a moment of happiness. There was a warm feeling of satisfaction in the letter itself. Just a casual dinner and the chance to talk as long as they wanted: giving such an invitation was the height of worldly pleasure to him.

A Free Piano Concert

Robert Schumann, student and future composer,
writing a letter to a friend

ZWICKAU, GERMANY · DECEMBER 1, 1827

On Saturday last I went with Walther and Rescher to Schneeberg [a mountain town in Saxony]. On Sunday, at about four, we started to come back, and came in for the most abominable weather. The snow was a yard deep, and no track had as yet been trodden out; one after the other we fell into the ditch by the roadside, which could hardly be distinguished from the road itself. When we arrived at Haslau [outside Zwickau], shivering and frozen, of course we first of all consumed some roast pork and pickled cucumber. We had a little money left, so we each of us ordered a large tumbler of grog; then we got excited, had a drinking bout of three, and sang student songs. The room was full of peasants [. . .] At last Walther told the peasants that I played the piano very well, etc.—in short, we gave a regular musico-dramatic soiree. I improvised freely upon "Fridolin." The rustics sat open-mouthed, when I was flourishing about on the keys in such a crazy manner. This over, a jolly little dance was got up, and we whirled the peasant girls about in rare style [. . .] We arrived at Zwickau after 12, still reeling and tottering about. It was indeed a most jovial evening, worthy of a Van Dyck!!

◦◦◦

Robert Schumann, who became one of the great Romantic composers, was born in 1810 in Zwickau (Saxony). In 1827, he was still attending school at the Zwickau Gymnasium. His father had noticed and encouraged his musical talent, but when he left school the following year it was to study law in Leipzig. His school friends, though, were already proud of his great talent as a performer on the piano. They helped him become a musician simply through their enjoyment of his gift.

He had been away with two of these friends, Walther and Rescher, for a hiking weekend to the town of Schneeberg, south of Zwickau. On the Sunday evening, as they were returning home, the weather worsened and they got caught in snow. Struggling on, they were wet and cold by the time they reached an inn at Haslau, outside Zwickau. They restored their sprits with a pleasant meal, and then they found they could still afford a drink of "grog." Soon they were in uproarious good humor, singing student songs together like a much larger company. Their friendship naturally found expression in a shared enjoyment of music.

The inn was "full of peasants"—this was evidently a place well favored by the locals. Robert's friend Walther could not resist telling the crowd that his companion "played the piano very well." Here was a young man who, one day, would command the great concert halls of Europe both with his compositions and as a soloist. Walther was proud of his friend, and this pride was a natural part of their mutual enjoyment of both life and music.

As Robert sat down at the inn's piano, a well-known tune ran through his head and he "improvised freely upon 'Fridolin.'" His fingers changed the melody, no doubt upside down, faster, slower, and every way. The other guests "sat open-mouthed," and he must have realized that, away from the strict world of school and home, he had found a real audience. It had taken a weekend away with friends to make this island of freedom and self-expression possible.

His astonishing performance finished, he was again able to be one of three student friends enjoying themselves on a winter evening in a warm inn. He, too, danced with the girls, presumably to the music played by the locals. Companionship gave him the confidence to explore his genius and then also welcomed him back into the simple, shared world of being young. They had arrived cold and weary; they departed for Zwickau very late, having had "a most jovial evening" together.

Garden

A Glad Return to the Old Pine Tree

Tao Yuanming, poet and retired official, composing a memoir

XUNYANG, CHINA · CA. 405 CE

Homewards I bend my steps. My fields, my gardens, are choked with weeds: should I not go? My soul has led a bondsman's life: why should I remain to pine? But I will waste no grief upon the past: I will devote my energies to the future. I have not wandered far astray. I feel that I am on the right track once again.

Lightly, lightly, speeds my boat along, my garments fluttering to the gentle breeze. I enquire my route as I go. I grudge the slowness of the dawning day. From afar I descry my old home, and joyfully press onwards in my haste. The servants rush forth to meet me; my children cluster at the gate. The place is a wilderness; but there is the old pine tree and my chrysanthemums. I take the little ones by the hand, and pass in. Wine is brought in full bottles, and I pour out in brimming cups. I gaze out at my favourite branches. I loll against the window in my newfound freedom. I look at the sweet children on my knee.

And now I take my pleasure in my garden. There is a gate, but it is rarely opened. I lean on my staff as I wander about or sit down to rest. I raise my head and contemplate the lovely scene. Clouds rise, unwilling, from the bottom of the hills: the weary bird seeks its nest again. Shadows vanish, but still I linger round my lonely pine. Home once more!

⟪◦∞◦⟫

Tao Yuanming was forty years old when he decided to abandon his moderately successful career as a minor provincial official and retire to his country home. He stayed there for the remainder of his days, more than twenty years. But Tao Yuanming was no mere bureaucrat. He was also a distinguished poet, whose work greatly gained in reputation over the centuries after his obscure life. This passage records the moment when he returned to the countryside, and it is typical of his unusually open and personal style.

His family had once been powerful and rich. But that had been two generations ago. He had inherited little, and he was returning that day to a simple home that was not in good shape. Early on, he felt this condition by lamenting the weeds covering the land.

But Tao Yuanming's mood soon brightened. His boat was almost home. He felt the breeze and sensed a fresh dawn. He glimpsed the old place, and then the household came rushing out to greet him. The sight of his children warmed him back to full life.

His garden was indeed neglected and overgrown. Yet he loved this place, which carried so many memories. There was the old pine tree, and also his chrysanthemums. The plants and the children went together in his sensibility, growing up in this safe and remote home, far from the corruption of court and bureaucracy.

The returned exile called for wine, and then he took in the garden scene, contemplating the many details—not just branches, for instance, but his "favourite branches."

Eventually the moment comes when he steps into his garden, to wander here and there among his many favored spots. He is completely at ease now, dwelling in his personal haven until the "shadows vanish."

There would be hard times ahead. Tao Yuanming knew that he was far from the wealth and comfort of the courts. Even a minor functionary in a city would have had an easier life than a farmer on a small country estate like this one. But that did not disturb the deep peace of the garden as it soaked into his soul.

After all the excitement of the return, he sat alone near his beloved pine tree, as if he was being welcomed back by the branches, the smells and sounds.

A Touch of Spring

Thomas Gray, poet and scholar, writing in his journal

CAMBRIDGE, CAMBRIDGESHIRE · MARCH 10, 1755

Wind S.W. Brisk, sunshine warm. Warm, hazy air all day till sunset. Mezereons bloom. Gooseberry and Elder put out their leaves. Apricots just show their blossom buds. Lesser Tortoiseshell Butterfly appears. Single Hepaticas in full bloom. First Violets blow, and Single Daffodils and Persian Iris.

∞

Thomas Gray lived alone in some rooms in Peterhouse, a Cambridge college. He was a shy man, nearly forty years old, who had begun to achieve fame as a poet, especially for his popular "Elegy Written in a Country Churchyard," a sadly reflective and beautiful poem about the shortness of life. He was a scholar of Latin and Greek who spent much of his time reading. He loved the college garden, and knew every bit of it.

The year so far had been cold. But now, on this early March day, he found the wind blowing nicely from the southwest and everything welcoming. The air had changed. It looked as different as it felt, and altogether it seemed that the sharpness of winter had passed. The lines and edges of things were softer: "Warm, hazy air all day till sunset." This sense of spring made the whole day into one extended happy moment in his favorite garden.

"Mezereons bloom. Gooseberry and Elder put out their leaves." These plants were not simply objects. To Gray, they were full of life. The purple mezereons were flowering into the warm spring air before his eyes. The first leaves on bushes and trees were unfolding as he watched them. The apricots were showing their buds on this very day. It was a moment of gentle rebirth.

Each moment seemed to bring a new gift: "Lesser Tortoiseshell Butterfly appears." It was as if small wonders were being conjured up by a magic spell. The garden was coming back to life one flower at a time: "Single Daffodils."

Yet at the same time, as a promise of all that would soon come, there was also the "full bloom" of the Hepaticas, small perennial flowers that had the strength to flourish at the very end of the winter cold. Their cycle of bloom was completing as other plants were just beginning. He was looking at the wonderful intricacy of time itself in this miniature of the natural world, forever consummated and reborn.

On this March 10 in a Cambridge garden, Thomas Gray perceived every leaf and flower as a distinct and separate creation. There were no general categories. "Hepaticas" now meant only these few lilac flowers, and the "Butterfly" named only one particular, fluttering speck of color. Words themselves were being reborn in that warm sunshine. In his happiness, it seemed as if the English language had been created to describe just this one day.

His delight in the "Lesser Tortoiseshell" was both that of a naturalist and a lover of passing moments. His passion for the world as it appeared in front of his eyes was paired with observant objectivity. He wanted to describe precisely this scene, as if to record it for eternity—although it would never exist again, either for him or for anyone else, exactly as it was on this one March day.

A year later, Gray moved to another Cambridge college, Pembroke. This was to be his last year in the college garden to which he was so attached. This warm early spring day was a lovely beginning to the finale.

Floral Abundance

Mary Dawson-Damer, aristocratic traveler,
writing in her diary

CAIRO · DECEMBER 31, 1841

*We made a detour to visit the mosque of Amurath. We returned to our hotel,
where we found some crazy-looking English carriages, in waiting to convey us
to the garden of Schoubra, a distance of about a league, through an avenue of
fine acacias, which in this climate are trees of considerable size, and afforded
us delightful shade from the glare and dust. The pods of these acacias are of
the size of tamarinds. I never saw anything to be compared to the beauty of
the Schoubra garden. It is quite an illustration of those described in the Arabian nights. It is formed in the original Grecian plan of garden: straight rows,
but thickly planted, and covering three square miles in extent. The lemon,
orange, myrtle, and pomegranate succeeded to and touched each other, and
below these, hedges of geranium in bright and full flower; the whole garden
appeared to have been just watered, and produced the most refreshing and yet
not overpowering fragrance.*

*We felt quite revived and enchanted, and might be excused for our constant
and repeated terms of admiration, of "Oh! how sweet!—Oh! how charming!"
Tired as I was on arriving, I soon felt quite restored with the effect of so balmy
an atmosphere.*

⁂

Mary Dawson-Damer and her husband, George, a middle-aged aristocratic couple from England, were traveling in Greece, Turkey,
Egypt, and Palestine. He was a cabinet minister in the British government. Her father had been a lord of the admiralty and a distinguished
sailor, as well as a friend of royalty. The Dawson-Damers lived a
metropolitan life at home in London.

She knew that "the garden of Schoubra" was part of the tourist
trail. Benjamin Disraeli, the novelist and future British prime minister, had visited there in 1830. He recorded his favorable impressions
of the man who had revived the garden, Muhammad Ali, the founder

of what became Egypt's ruling dynasty until 1952. This garden was also the site of his palace.

The couple got into the waiting carriages as usual to go and see another sight. First signs were promising; a fine avenue of trees provided relief "from the glare and dust." Nothing, though, prepared Mary Dawson-Damer for the sight of the garden itself: "I never saw anything to be compared to the beauty" of this Eden. It was like a scene from the *Arabian Nights*, as if she had entered a mythical realm.

Initially, she was impressed by its sheer size, three square miles of colorful trees, shrubs, and flowers. On such a large scale, as a lush landscape that was carefully arranged, she appreciated the open, "straight rows" of the planting. It was a kind of classical order that she called "Grecian," though in fact the country she was presently touring was the origin of this geometric vision, since Pythagoras had derived some of his main ideas from Egyptian sources. Wave after wave of "lemon, orange, myrtle, and pomegranate" trees, with their different colors and smells, "touched each other," and even the space below the trees was planted with geraniums "in bright and full flower."

Yet even that profusion was not quite why Mary Dawson-Damer had such a sensation of intense happiness at the garden of Schoubra. The whole place seemed to have just been watered. After all the dust and heat, her senses were met by a misty cloud, filled with the scents of every kind of plant surrounding her. It was the distillation of sweetness. Her pleasure was both sensory and spiritual, as she was breathing in the essence of this garden.

The Hours before Dawn at the Imperial Court

Murasaki Shikibu, author and court lady,
writing in her diary

KYOTO, JAPAN · CA. 1008–1010

Each treetop around the pond, each tuft of grass by the stream, takes on its own colour, which becomes more alluring in the charming light of the sky. Even more moving is the monks' ceaseless recitation of the sutras. Against the sound of the gradually cooling breeze, it blends with the endless trickling of the water throughout the night [. . .]

It is still the depth of night. Clouds obscure the moon, and dark shadows lie beneath the trees. Voices are heard: "How about we open the shutters?" "But the ladies probably won't be ready yet!" "Attendant! Open the shutters!"

Suddenly the bell that announces the Ritual of the Five Great Mystic Kings is rung, and the pre-dawn ceremony begins. The clamour of the priests' voices vying with one another is heard near and far; it is truly magnificent.

The abbot of the Kannon-in hall leads twenty priests out from the east wing to recite incantations. Even their footsteps as they stomp across the bridge sound strange. When the head priest of Hosshoji Temple returns to the stables, and the head of Henji Temple to the library, I imagine looking over at them as they cross those elegant arched bridges, accompanied by their retinues robed in priestly attire, and disappear among the trees. What a moving sight! [. . .] Dawn breaks as the men and women of the court assemble.

As I look out through my door into the faint mist, I see that the morning dew is still on the leaves.

⌘

Known only by her nickname, "Murasaki Shikibu," this court lady was the author of the famous romance *The Tale of Genji*, written at the Japanese court at the beginning of the eleventh century. Her story of Prince Genji quickly became a cult among the courtiers of the imperial palace in Kyoto, where she was an attendant to the empress. Murasaki's family was distantly related to the dominant branch of the Fujiwara clan, whose chief, Michinaga, was the real power in the empire. She, though, was on the fringe of the hierarchy, living in the part of the inner palace reserved for attendant women.

Her real name is lost. "Murasaki," meaning purple or lavender, is the name of one of the female characters in her romance, and "Shikibu" was her father's rank in the imperial service. Leading up to the year 1010, she was probably in her late thirties, a widow with a daughter, passionately loyal to a mistress who was herself insecure in that palace of intrigue and rivalry.

Late one night, she was looking out on the garden of the palace. The outlines of the trees appeared as strange and beautiful objects faintly outlined in the dim glow of the night sky. Even the clusters of grass were patches of dark colors along the water. This garden was both a place of beauty and a sacred space, where many temples were scattered. Bridges led over streams and ponds.

Then Murasaki hears the chanting of the monks and the music of the water merge into one voice, calling from the heart of this mysterious night. But these mundane interruptions do not break the spell. The very start of the day's ceremonies is in preparation, still under the cover of night. A bell rings. The Ritual of the Five Great Mystic Kings puts to flight threatening spirits of evil and so makes each day safe. This ritual is the prelude to first light.

Those were the rules and conventions. But for the listening woman, the bell, the voices, and the water created a musical moment she found "truly magnificent." She heard, as if for the first time, the sound of the monks' footsteps as they crossed a bridge. Every noise was distinct. She noticed other clergy, crossing bridges and walking along paths. Morning was creeping through the garden.

As night and dawn met, she had another moment of pure beauty, glimpsing through "the faint mist" a sparkling garden of "morning dew."

Perfect Fragrance

Ogier Ghiselin de Busbecq, diplomat,
writing a letter to a friend

NEAR ISTANBUL · WINTER OF 1554/55

After stopping one day at Adrianople [Edirne], we set out to finish the last stage of our journey to Constantinople [Istanbul], which is not far distant. As we passed through these districts we were presented with large nosegays of flowers, the narcissus, the hyacinth, and the tulipan (as the Turks call this last). We were very much surprised to see them blooming in midwinter, a season which does not suit flowers at all. There is a great abundance of the narcissus and hyacinth in Greece; their fragrance is perfectly wonderful, so much so that, when in great profusion, they affect the heads of those who are unaccustomed to the scent. The tulip has little or no smell; its recommendation is the variety and beauty of the colouring.

⁕

Ogier Ghiselin de Busbecq was born in 1522 in Flanders. He was a talented youngster who entered the University of Louvain at the age of thirteen. He was the illegitimate son of a local landowner, but such was his progress that the authorities issued a patent for his legitimacy. In November 1554, at a comparatively young age, Busbecq became the ambassador for the Holy Roman emperor to the court of the Ottoman sultan at Constantinople. War was in the air, and his task was to negotiate as good a truce as he could manage.

On the way to Turkey, Busbecq met his predecessor coming home—whose reminiscences were not encouraging. He had been kept a virtual prisoner (and the severity of the conditions would mean that he died before reaching his native soil again). It was going to be a hard time at the sultan's court.

The journey was in itself a long and difficult one, having all the anxiety of anticipation to contend with as well. Yet at "the last stage," Busbecq was still awake to his surroundings. The locals approached them "with large nosegays of flowers." This land seemed to have become one huge garden. Everywhere the flowers bloomed, and especially so "the narcissus, the hyacinth, and the tulipan."

In fact, Busbecq wrote these letters at a later time, as a kind of memoir. They were addressed to his friend Nicholas Michault, a fellow diplomat. It may be that the description of the flowers blooming all around did not belong to that winter journey at all. He did visit this region at other times, when the flowers might more obviously have been flourishing. The ambiguous chronology only serves to emphasize the vividness of the impressions themselves. Perhaps he could not remember exactly when he had those experiences of the narcissus, hyacinths, and tulips. But he remembered perfectly what it felt like to encounter this land of gardens.

First there was the color, "to see them blooming" far and wide. Then there was "their fragrance," so sweet and strong that it was "perfectly wonderful." He recalled vividly the wave of scent as it met his senses. It was enough to make a man feel as if drunk!

The happiness of that moment was independent really of anything around it. This was the "great profusion" of the earth, reaching all of the human senses.

Busbecq knew about many of these flowers from classical literature if not from personal experience. But the tulip was new to him. At first, it seemed less fine than the narcissus and hyacinth because it had "little or no smell." But the coloring was supreme, and there were so many shades of tulips!

Before all the negotiations and threats, there was this very human moment. For a European diplomat in the sixteenth century, the world often seemed like a vast battlefield, with armies maneuvering back and forth. But here, one man was able to see the land as a garden, and conversation as an exchange between people who loved the flowers growing there.

It took eight years for Busbecq to negotiate a viable truce. For much of that time, he was confined to the embassy in Constantinople. Yet such interludes of vividness, such glimpses of fragrance and color, were the true human legacy of a difficult decade in his life. The moments of happiness outlived the years of fear and struggle.

The Pleasant Distraction of a Blooming Greenhouse

William Cowper, poet, writing a letter to a friend

OLNEY, BUCKINGHAMSHIRE · JUNE 8, 1783

Our severest winter, commonly called the spring, is now over, and I find myself seated in my favourite recess, the greenhouse. In such a situation, so silent, so shady, where no human foot is heard, and where only my myrtles presume to peep in at the window, you may suppose I have no interruption to complain of, and that my thoughts are perfectly at my command. But the beauties of the spot are themselves an interruption, my attention being called upon by those very myrtles, by a double row of grass pinks just beginning to blossom, and by a bed of beans already in bloom; and you are to consider it, if you please, as no small proof of my regard, that though you have so many powerful rivals, I disengage myself from them all, and devote this hour entirely to you.

⁓⧫⁓

William Cowper had a stormy and often unhappy life. Born in 1731, the son of an English clergyman, he had become a London lawyer, which did not fit his shy temperament. Unhappiness in love added to his natural melancholy, and in 1763 he attempted suicide. From this depression he was rescued by the friendship of the Unwin family. After Mr. Unwin died following a riding accident in 1767, Cowper, the widowed Mary Unwin, and her children moved together to the peaceful village of Olney near Huntingdon in eastern England. Cowper was a close friend of the Olney curate John Newton, who wrote the words of the hymn "Amazing Grace." Despite this supportive environment, the poet suffered another serious collapse in 1773.

Then he discovered the two passions of his life. One was poetry, which he began to publish to great acclaim. The second was gardening. He cultivated melons in this greenhouse and was proud of the hotbed of cucumbers. He loved talking to professional gardeners and exchanging tips on planting. Now he was sitting in the greenhouse writing to his friend William Unwin, Mary's son.

Spring was just ending. For William Cowper, it was a season of false hopes. To him, it was impossible to enjoy the garden when spring showers and chills were never far away. Now he had an early English summer day, and he could be confident that nothing would go wrong: "Our severest winter, commonly called the spring, is now over." He was able to joke about the poor spring, though, with his low spirits, he really needed sunshine and warmth.

He felt as if he had just woken from a troubled sleep: "I find myself seated in my favourite recess, the greenhouse." He had other hiding places, but this was his chosen spot. The greenhouse was his haven, a retreat from the dangers and difficulties of life. He was safe here, almost invisible, where "no human foot is heard, and where only my myrtles presume to peep in at the window." He felt as if even the flowers were careful not to intrude on him.

It was not only the outer world that felt safe inside the greenhouse. Even more important, his mind was at peace here. He could think the thoughts that he wanted, unpressurized by worries—"my thoughts are perfectly at my command." Tranquil feelings seemed to soothe his mind in the warm, quiet place where he was sitting. Often, in his troubled days, he had been unable to choose his thoughts in this peaceful way. To have his mind "perfectly at my command" was for William Cowper a moment of absolute happiness.

The only "interruption" from these chosen reflections was the sheer beauty of nature, the colors and shapes surrounding him. But he did not really want to avoid such distraction. Here both the outer and the inner world were welcoming and he was secure. For once at rest in mind and soul, he could write to his friend.

The Manmade Rainbow

Michel de Montaigne, philosopher, writing in his travel diary

TIVOLI, ITALY · APRIL 4, 1581

In Tivoli is to be seen the famous palace [Villa d'Este] and garden of the cardinal of Ferrara, a most exquisite piece of work [. . .]

This outburst of a countless number of jets of water [in the garden], turned on or off by a single appliance manipulated at some distant point, I had seen elsewhere during my travels, notably at Florence and Augsburg, as I have already recorded. Here real music is produced from a sort of natural organ, which always plays the same tune, by the means of water which falls with great force into a round vaulted recess where it disturbs the air and forces it to seek an exit, and at the same time supplies the wind necessary to make the organ pipes sound. Another stream of water turns a wheel fitted with teeth, which are set so as to strike in a certain order the keyboard of the organ, and the sound of trumpets is also counterfeited by the same agency [. . .]

There are many pools or reservoirs edged all round with stone balustrades, on the top of which are set divers high columns of stone, distant one from the other about four paces. From the summits of these pillars the water spouts forth with strong impetus, not upward, but down towards the water in the basin. All the jets, being turned inwards and facing one another, discharge the water into the tank with such velocity that, when the threads of water collide in the air, they let descend into the basin a thick and continual mist. The sun falling upon the same produces on the surface of the basin, in the air, and all round about, a rainbow so marked and so like nature that it in no way falls short of the bow seen in the sky. I saw nought to equal this elsewhere.

❧

Michel de Montaigne was born near Bordeaux, in southwest France, in 1533. After many years of private study in philosophy and literature, he became a notable writer and philosopher, famed especially for his development of the essay as a literary form. In 1580, he published to great acclaim two volumes of these essays, and also went on a tour round Europe, partly to try and revive his failing health (he had kidney stones). He kept a diary, which he did not intend to publish (though it enhanced his posthumous reputation when it was made public more than a century later). These were his private notes of a time intended for recovery and renewal.

The Villa d'Este in Tivoli, near Rome, was one of the masterpieces of Italian Renaissance garden design, equipped with the latest cunning technology. These water-powered machines were precursors of the Industrial Age, even though in this garden they were only toys.

Montaigne enjoyed the craft and ingenuity of the waterworks and contraptions. But he was only really stirred to passion by one sight. This was something special, worth the visit even when he was not really feeling well.

Toward the end of his garden tour, he noticed a kind of "upside-down" fountain, with jets firing the water down into the basin instead of throwing it up into the air. The result was an artificial mist, a fine cloud of watery vapor, enabling the sunlight to create a magnificent rainbow. Now this was something—a rainbow machine! It fitted Montaigne's idea of happiness. Unlike the other machinery, which tried to compete with nature, this fountain was—intentional or not—a tribute to the unsurpassable beauty of the real rainbow.

Only at this spot in the great Renaissance garden, Montaigne must have felt, were nature and human creation in true harmony. What better than rainbows to bloom in this Italian masterpiece!

Flowers and Fruits Blaze for a Birthday

Oliver Wendell Holmes, poet and physician, writing a letter to three friends

BEVERLY FARMS, MASSACHUSETTS · SEPTEMBER 2, 1885

My dear Friends—I cannot make phrases in thanking you for your kind remembrance. I wish you could all have been with me on the 29th [of August, his birthday]; every flower of garden and greenhouse, and fruits that Paradise would not have been ashamed of, embowered and emblazoned our wayside dwelling.

Grow old, my dear Boys, grow old! Your failings are forgotten, your virtues are overrated, there is just enough of pity in the love that is borne you to give it a tenderness all its own. The horizon line of age moves forward by decades. At sixty, seventy seems to bound the landscape; at seventy, the eye rests on the line of eighty; at eighty, we can see through the mist and still in the distance a ruin or two of ninety; and if we reach ninety, the mirage of our possible centennial bounds our prospect.

❧

Oliver Wendell Holmes had been a distinguished physician, a professor of anatomy and dean at Harvard University. He was a pioneer of the successful theory of infectious diseases. Yet he was also a well-known poet and acclaimed public speaker. Now he was writing a letter to three equally distinguished friends—James Russell Lowell, Charles Eliot Norton, and George William Curtis, who were themselves writers, academics, and public figures—about an experience on his seventy-sixth birthday, a few days previously.

He was currently staying at his summer home in Beverly Farms, a pleasant and fashionable coastal resort not far from Boston. It was here that he generally celebrated his birthdays, often receiving an array of telegrams and letters. As he had grown older, he had declared to would-be visitors that he was "not at home" on the day, which he wanted to spend in rural peace.

He was feeling well. His life had been extremely successful. He had accomplished much, and had received various honors.

But now he was not thinking about his great achievements. Instead, being at peace with himself, he called to mind a moment from his birthday: "I wish you could all have been with me on the 29th; every flower of garden and greenhouse, and fruits that Paradise would not have been ashamed of, embowered and emblazoned our wayside dwelling." It must have been a beautiful late summer day, as the season along the shore was coming to an end.

He had achieved great status in academia and culture. But his summer house, where he could be at peace, made him happy without any further acclaim or fuss. He was glad that the flowers and trees graced his world there.

As he was writing this letter, he recalled with great joy the momentary surge of all that green and color, greeting his elderly senses as fresh and full as ever. He had the added pleasure of reflection: "Grow old, my dear Boys, grow old!" In a way, it was the word "grow" that connected this ironic advice (what choice was there?) to the blazing display of the birthday blooms. People and plants shared this creative principle.

In the prime of his life, he had been successful on many fronts, sometimes against strong opposition, as when he defended the germ theory of infection. Now he felt that as an old man, he might be accepted simply for being still in this world; and so he could enjoy the pleasures of each passing moment, almost as if it were his last, but without fear or regret.

Family

The Sweet Thought of the Children

Yamanoue no Okura, poet and official, composing a poem

KYOTO, JAPAN · CA. 700 CE

When I eat melon
My children come to mind;
When I eat crisp chestnuts
All the stronger is my love for them.
Oh, whence do they come
Time after time present in my thoughts?
How can I just fall asleep soundly?

❦

Yamanoue no Okura was a scholar and official living at the Japanese imperial court in Kyoto. He was middle-aged and a distinguished scholar at a time when scholarship brought political status. In his later career, he became an envoy to China and a provincial governor. But when he wrote about his feelings, his career was not the most important part of his life. When he tried to express what made him feel good to be alive on this earth, he ignored the grandeur of court life, the honors and the ceremonies. He said nothing about wealth or power. Instead, he talked about the joy that his children had given him. Compared with that, the rest was insignificant.

Here he captured two moments that were extremely simple. First there was the joy of eating melon. When he tasted this fruit, his children were present to him with the same sweetness. Then there were "crisp chestnuts," a favorite treat of Japanese autumns. The sweetness of the chestnuts brought the love for his children harmoniously to mind. They were the sweetest part of his life, and his poem enabled him to convey how he felt when he was mindful of them: it was like the taste of the best fruit in the world.

The fact of his children's existence was more intense because they themselves were not with him right now. The wonder of having these children blended with the astonishment that the world had such sweet flavors to offer. Not only did melon and chestnut exist, but they were

57

part of everyday life. It took no struggle or chance to come upon them. They were not the spoils of war or the rewards of toil. They were free blessings. The flavor of life flowed like love.

What makes the children "time after time present in my thoughts," Yamanoue no Okura wondered. What was the deep and hidden source of such blessing, the secret spring from which the river of life arose and flowed into people's lives? The curiosity was part of the happiness of these moments. He was a very reflective man, and questions were like melon and chestnuts to him—they opened in his mind with a sweet taste.

His curiosity, his feelings, had led him to explore philosophy more widely than was common at the imperial court. Reaching beyond the Buddhist values that were orthodox there, he discovered the power of the Chinese thinker Confucius, with his distinctive emphasis on family love.

Sometimes the stream of his children's images was so vivid that it would not let him go to sleep at night. This was the passionate sense of life itself, too full of energy for the mind to sink into slumber. In those nighttime hours, his joy was surely mixed with longing.

When he had that tang of melon and chestnut in his mouth, his children seemed present, immediately. It was this sense of closeness, the reality of his love for these children, that gave Yamanoue no Okura true moments of happiness.

An Outing to the Park

Charlotte Bousfield, engineer's wife, writing in her diary

BEDFORD, BEDFORDSHIRE · AUGUST 3, 1879

In the afternoon all of us except Ted went to Ampthill Park and had tea in it. John rode the bicycle in turn with Will, and Papa and myself with the girls and Florence rode and walked by turns; the afternoon was delightful and we thoroughly enjoyed our meal in the open air.

⌒∞⌒

The first Monday of August was a public holiday in Victorian Britain, and it was a fine, sunny one in 1879 in the town of Bedford, north of London. Charlotte Bousfield, a middle-aged woman, was taking her family for an outing. Her husband, Edward ("Papa"), was a successful engineer with one of the leading manufacturers of farming machinery.

The eldest son, Will, had graduated from Cambridge University in mathematics. He was now becoming a patent lawyer in Bristol, having acquired his father's interest in new inventions. He was in his mid-twenties. With him on that day was his wife, Florence. They had married that April, and this was their first proper visit to his parents as a wedded couple. The second-eldest brother, Ted, a recently qualified doctor, was missing because he had to be at work. The youngest, John, was in his early twenties and lived with family friends in the Essex town of Chelmsford, so he, too, was home on a visit. There were two daughters: Lottie, who at seventeen had just left school and was being trained by her mother in the domestic skills required to run a Victorian household, and Hattie, thirteen and still at school.

The Bousfields went to a country estate near Bedford, Ampthill Park, where the grounds were open for people to enjoy themselves. They took turns riding a bicycle. The two young men, being faster, were haring off first, the others taking their turns.

Victorian families have the reputation of having been rigid. On that August holiday, the Bousfields were at ease: husband and wife, older and younger, they all shared the same enjoyment.

The love of cycling went with a liking for new machines and gadgets, a professional field for Papa and Will and a shared enthusiasm for Charlotte, the mother. Yet in another way, the openness of the air and the parkland setting were an antidote to the industrious pattern of their normal days. Ampthill had been a royal residence long ago, and the park had been laid out by the eighteenth-century master designer Capability Brown. His liking for romantic vistas meant that it was perfect for cycling and strolling, without needing to arrive anywhere. That was no doubt one reason for the relaxed way they were able to take turns. These were busy folk who did not normally have time to dawdle and linger. Their days were usually driven by purpose.

This afternoon blossomed into happiness when they had a picnic together. There is a lovely sense of a shared experience in "our meal," the picnic that they liked to take with them on such outings. Back then, there was almost something daring about having a meal "in the open air." They were shaking off the constraints of convention that governed everyday life rather tightly.

Yet this was also an expression of their essential personalities. Charlotte Bousfield's chosen words, "thoroughly enjoyed," capture how this happiness grew out of their way of living. Everything they did, this family did thoroughly. So they experienced this glimpse of leisure as fully as they committed themselves to the rhythms of work.

For Will and Florence, this was an afternoon of being warmly received as a married couple. Her new mother-in-law had been friendly and supportive to Florence during the engagement, and it must have been pleasant for the newlyweds to spend such a relaxed holiday afternoon. While Victorian family life was often very formal, here the casual setting and the shared recreation made for a genuine ease and enjoyment together.

Pride in an Unfinished New Home

Tryphena White, daughter of a settler family,
writing in her diary

CAMILLUS, NEW YORK · AUGUST 5, 1805

Monday, we washed in rain water which we caught a few days before, and baked, and in the afternoon we began to move our little all over the river to our new building; we got our things chiefly over, at least those things which we wanted most to keep house with, and I went up [the steps to the] chamber and made up the beds on the floor. Polly came over to help me [. . .] The building is something like our shop, there is two rooms in it, and the chimney is right in the middle of the house, or is to be, for it is not built yet, the lower floor is all in one room, and a joiner's table in one end of it, and a joiner at work. We have some shelves made to put our crockery etc. on, and a trap door to go down [into the] cellar with, and just one half of our chamber floor laid, and that with loose rough boards, we have 4 beds down, 2 one side of the room and 2 the other. My bed I have partitioned off with a curtain. We have a place made out a little way from the house to hang on a pot and kettle, and we do our cooking there. It is very customary for people here to keep their fire outdoors, when they have a fire place, but we feel as proud of our house, as inconvenient as it is, as ever any person did of the most elegant house in the world.

⚬❧⚬

The White family moved from their longtime home in West Springfield, Massachusetts, to a new settlement in upstate New York. Camillus was hardly a village yet, just a few houses and the beginnings of a square. Tryphena White's father, Joseph, was building a small house in Genesee Street, where a few others already stood; he also had a water mill built nearby.

Tryphena White was in her early twenties. Her brother Elijah was still at home, and her older sister, Anna, together with her husband, had also moved to Camillus. The children's mother had died many years before, and they now had an affectionate stepmother called Phebe (Phoebe).

In June 1805, Tryphena White had recorded the beginning of the construction of their new home: "Saturday in the afternoon our building was raised." For the meantime, they had to camp, and conditions were difficult. On this Monday morning in August, they "washed in rain water," which they had stored from the rainfall a few days ago, and also did some baking. The afternoon was very special: "We began to move our little all." She had been looking forward to this day for a long time, coping with the primitive conditions and the lack of privacy. They went "over the river," where the water mill would be built, and arrived at their new home.

Immediately, she began to sort things out. Her steps may have echoed on the wooden stairs as she climbed up to the bedchamber for the first time. They had brought some sheets and blankets, so she "made up the beds on the floor." She did not want to go back to the camp.

The next good thing was that her friend Polly arrived to keep her company. She was the daughter of Mrs. Reid, a neighbor who had been hospitably giving the White family tea for the past weeks.

Nothing was quite ready in the home, and Tryphena White recorded how the chimney, so crucial for the house, "is to be, for it is not built yet." Not only was the carpenter's table still downstairs, but so was the carpenter himself. She also pointed out the "loose rough boards," and there was nowhere to cook inside yet.

Yet as she took stock of this improvised beginning of her new life, she experienced a fierce surge of happiness, which she preserved with the declaration that "we feel as proud of our house, as inconvenient as it is, as ever any person did of the most elegant house in the world." She was happy to be one of the White family, with their resilience and their optimism, as they made their new start in this settlement that was still young in itself. It was the middle of the summer, and finally they were home.

Together Again, At Last

Du Fu, poet, writing a poem

QIANG VILLAGE, CHINA • CA. 758 CE

The sunset reddens o'er the lofty peak.
The sun steps down the level plain to seek.

The sparrows twitter on the wicker door
Home! yet so many miles have left me weak.

My wife and children start to see me here.
Surprise scarce vanquished wipes a furtive tear:

To think that swept by anarchy away
Yet Chance returns me to each bosom dear.

⁓∞⁓

One of the most celebrated Chinese poets, Du Fu was born in 712 CE, during the long rule of the Tang dynasty. The world he grew up in was relatively stable, but during his lifetime this fabric became torn. This deeply personal passage from a little poem records a moment of joy from these dangerous and difficult years.

Despite his immense gifts, Du Fu failed the civil service examination that gave access to official careers. His last—and failed—attempt was in 747, and so he never really prospered under the rigid rules of the time. In the early 750s he married and had a family. After that, he developed a uniquely personal approach to poetry, writing about ordinary life and the troubles and pleasures of common people.

Meanwhile, the empire became less secure as the hitherto invincible Tang armies were defeated by foreign powers along the threatened borders, and an internal revolt became the full-scale An Lushan rebellion in 755. The emperor had to flee the capital at Chang'an. Du Fu, too, fled northwards with his family. At one point, his wife and children carried on, but he was unable to follow. He was captured by the rebels and was returned to the capital, where he became trapped.

Eventually he escaped and traveled alone down the long road to the emperor's court at Fengxiang.

He had been separated from his family for a long time, and when the court granted him a family visit, he walked two hundred miles to try and find them. He had survived all the loneliness and worry. And now there was this moment of returning home—he had found his family at last. It was like a miracle to see his loved ones in the huge turmoil that had gripped the country.

This poem was written after Du Fu's reunion with his family in around 758 at the village of Qiang. The moment was defined by the light of sunset. The war-torn land he had crossed was redeemed on this evening. The perspective stretched, like the image of memory, all the way to the horizon under a reddening sky. Over there was the big world that—for now—he had left behind.

Ahead of him was home. His gaze rested on small things—a wicker door, and sparrows chirping. This small scale moved him because he had been stranded in a world of vast spaces and impersonal distances. Now he had returned to the life he used to lead. Here and now this particular gate mattered because it was his. Here his wife and children, as well as these sparrows, had their home.

Now he could look back over the "level plain" where he had traveled to be with his family once again. He could still feel the hardships of his journey. He had had his share of bad fortune, but now luck had favored him in the best way possible. He could feel how much this reunion also meant to his wife and their children, seeing him suddenly emerge from the perilous world beyond. Their tears, barely suppressed, contained the intensity of their joyful relief.

He continued the poem with another glimpse of this peaceful local world: "The garden wall with neighbours' heads is lined. / Each breast surcharging breaks in sighings kind."

Deep Gratitude for Health

John Hull, silversmith and businessman, writing in his diary

BOSTON · SUMMER OF 1658

7th of 7th [July]. My cousin Daniel Quincy was also cast upon his sick-bed, within a week after the other [Robert Sanderson's son, John], and had also the fever, and was brought very low, but, through God's favour, well recovered by the 17th of 8th [August]. My wife was ill when these [two] first began to be sick: but it pleased God, as they sickened, she strengthened; and He kept her, and my little daughter Hannah, that then sucked upon her, from any spice of the fever, though continually necessitated to be in the same chamber. The Lord make me sensible of his hand, and of the mixtures of his mercy to me therein, though most unworthy.

⚬⚬⚬

John Hull came to Boston from England with his parents in 1635, when he was about ten years old. He became a successful member of the Massachusetts colony, training as a silversmith and then being appointed mintmaster. In partnership with Robert Sanderson, he devised and made the first coinage for the Massachusetts mint. In 1647, he married Judith Quincy, from one of the leading families in Boston.

They had already lost children in infancy before "the fever" (probably the measles) came to the colony in 1658. He had watched the sickness getting closer to his own family: "My cousin Daniel Quincy was also cast upon his sick-bed, within a week after the other, and had also the fever." His wife became ill around the same time. It was a time of desperate fear.

Hull's wife, Judith, might have caught the illness from the others (although infection was not understood at that time). If the sickness did pass between people in that way, then he had also reason to worry about their child, "my little daughter Hannah." The baby could not be moved away from the mother since she was still being breast-fed. He was worried that some "spice of the fever" might pass to the baby. She was small and frail; how could she possibly survive when adults did sicken and die? His fear was vividly caught by the word "spice," which suggested that the merest little grain of the disease could be too much.

But his fear was proven groundless. Instead of disaster, there came recovery. His wife regained her health as "she strengthened," and their baby daughter had been kept safe from the scourge. He expressed the sudden happy relief as thanks to God: "The Lord make me sensible of his hand." For some time past, he must have been tormented by a fear of malign fate. Now he was able to feel thankful again for God's "mixtures of his mercy to me therein."

He felt that he had done nothing to deserve such blessings. That was part of the unspeakable joy that came to him, "though most unworthy."

Eighteen years later his daughter, Hannah, married the judge and writer Samuel Sewall. On her wedding day, John Hull is said to have given her an unusual dowry: her weight measured in his pine-tree coins, some of the first American colonial coinage.

Such deliverance from the ominous shadow of loss remains a profound part of all family love. The seventeenth-century father expressed his joy with careful dignity, which did not hide the depth of the fear and the profound gratitude he felt as that darkened summer passed.

A Father's Gift of Fruit and Sugar

Edmund Verney, wealthy gentleman, writing a letter to his son

LONDON · JANUARY 22, 1685

I have this day sent you [. . .] all your things except your old coat, which I did not think you would need nor worth sending; your old hat I did not send neither, for it was so bad I was ashamed of it. All your new things I bought you I put into a new box [. . .] and your two guineas in your fob [small pocket], and a new knife and fork in your great pocket; and so God bless you, and send you well to do.

> *I am your loving father*
> *Edmund Verney*

> *In your trunk I have put for you*
> *18 Seville oranges*
> *6 Malaga lemons*
> *3 pounds of brown sugar*
> *1 pound of white powdered sugar made up in quarters*
> *1 lb of brown sugar candy*
> *¼ of a lb of white sugar candy*
> *1 lb of picked raisins, good for a cough*
> *4 nutmegs.*

Edmund Verney was nearly fifty years old. He had lost his wife many years before. His son, also named Edmund, had left the day before by coach from their home in London to return to studying at Oxford University. The whole of that day had been spent packing, and now the luggage was to follow him.

The Verneys were a wealthy and important family. They had large estates in Buckinghamshire, where Sir Ralph, Edmund senior's father, was the landowner. Sir Ralph had been an important politician in the reign of King Charles I, but he had run into difficulty during and after the Civil War that ended with the execution of the king in 1649. Oliver Cromwell came to power and the monarchy was temporarily replaced by the Commonwealth. Sir Ralph had taken his family into exile in France, even being imprisoned on their return to England. But since the Restoration of the monarchy under Charles II in 1660, the Verneys had been secure again in the old prosperity. Still, Edmund senior had known troubles.

There were plenty of servants in their London home to do the packing and sorting. He did not need to do this work himself. It was his choice. His feeling of loving care showed through his words.

He carefully sorted out his son's belongings. With a touch of humor, he reported his decision to withhold the "old coat," and also the battered hat that went with it. He carefully listed the two guineas, the new knife and fork, and "a new box" to put various purchases in. "God bless you," he added warmly. "I am your loving father."

Then he put in some treats: oranges and lemons, not easy to come by in an English winter. They were luxury items, certainly. Sugar had begun to become part of English everyday life, but to the more familiar brown sugar he added some fine embellishments: fancy cubes, some candy, raisins and nutmegs, and spice from the Indies. There was a hint of concern in his reminder that the raisins were "good for a cough."

Edmund Verney's love and happiness as a father were expressed in these lines, particularly in words like "In your trunk I have put for you." Aristocrats like him really did not do these things themselves. But he *did*, putting in the sugar and fruit, choosing little precious gifts—"for you."

It was well judged. In the son's carefully kept accounts, very little is spent for wine, but there are frequently small entries for "Oranges, Apples, Sugar Plums and Spice."

Kings come and go (Charles II was dying), but the human heart lives on in such private moments.

The Loving Presence of Her Children

Hannah Mary Rathbone, looking after her
dying mother-in-law, writing in her journal

NEAR LIVERPOOL · APRIL 1839

While dressing, my mother[-in-law] said, "I have a sharp pain in my head, but it is going off." I tried to help her to dress, and she said I could help her if I could only tell her what she wanted.

After breakfast I was reading to her in Bishop Wilson's Sacra Privata *[book by Bishop Thomas Wilson], the Wednesday morning meditations. Observing that she pressed her hands against her head, I asked if I should leave off; she made no reply, and I took her hand and begged her to lie down. She said "Yes," but did not attempt to move, and seemed unable to collect her thoughts, repeating the word "Yes." She seemed much distressed and kept feeling with her hands, saying, "Who, who?" [. . .]*

Love and affection for her family seemed to fill her whole heart and mind. Once, when I thought she wished me to leave the room, she turned to me and said, "Thee, I never wish thee to leave the room," and putting her face close to mine, whispered, "I wish thee always to be in the room."

On her own daughter Hannah entering the bedroom, "Is this Hannah, my Hannah? Oh that is a comfort." Again, on hearing the voice of her son Richard, "Is not that my dear Dicky's voice? Bless him, bless him, bless him," adding slowly and distinctly, "Thy will be done as it is in Heaven." Another time to me, "Hannah Mary, oh my dear child, how didst thou get here? Do get me some pocket handkerchiefs, I have been so in want of them." To her son, "Richard, dear Richard," and as he stooped down to her she kissed him very affectionately, and putting his hand to her lips kissed it several times.

She expressed great thankfulness for all the kindness of her children, saying, "All has been done that can be done."

⁂

Hannah Mary Rathbone had come with her husband, Richard, and their small child to stay with her elderly mother-in-law at the Rathbone country estate Greenbank, outside Liverpool. Originally, they had come to escape the works going on at their own home in Liverpool, where Richard was a successful merchant: "Richard and I and the baby came to stay at the Cottage [Greenbank] while our own house was being painted." It started off as a pleasant stay, but there was a shadow: "April 2, 1839. We moved down to the Cottage. Several days passed very comfortably, and we enjoyed ourselves very much, but I was greatly struck with my mother[-in-law]'s increased feebleness."

Richard's mother, also called Hannah Mary, had been ill for some time. She had lived a rich life here at Greenbank, the beloved home for her and her family. Her husband had died many years before, but the house had remained a center for family and community.

Now she was in pain and increasingly cut off from the world, "unable to collect her thoughts." But the deepest feelings of her life remained strong: "Love and affection for her family."

These were the emotions that had motivated and enriched the older Hannah Mary's whole life. Now they found their final expression in moments of deep human contact as she was losing her bearings in the world, simple moments like "putting her face close to mine." In the gathering mist, her loving bond remained: "Is this Hannah, my Hannah? Oh that is a comfort," she said, and also: "Is not that my dear Dicky's voice? Bless him, bless him, bless him." These bright bursts of recognition shone like a beam on the gathering family. In these moments, a fundamental happiness broke through, the flavor of a whole life lived to the full.

A Warm Welcome by the In-Laws

Ann Warder, wife of a businessman,
writing in her diary

PHILADELPHIA · JUNE 7, 1786

[June] 6th—At dinner a violent shower detained us long, but the good horses and no stopping soon carried us the twenty miles [to Philadelphia] where mother [John Warder's mother], Aunt Hooten [. . .], her husband, cousin John Hooten, the four Parkers and [John's] sister Emlen were impatiently awaiting our arrival, which they were not at all apprised of 'till I got upstairs, when it would not be in my power to do justice to all the joy and affection shown me. It was one hour and a half before my dearest [John] arrived owing to the fatigue of the poor cattle. My arrival had prepared dear mother for the pleasure she had so much anticipated—think then of her delight to see one who was always the darling, after ten years absence. The evening was spent with the family, sister Emlen, Billy and Sally Morris, and J. Fry [. . .]

[June] 7th—I rested well in mother's best bed, the room large and house spacious. Below are the shop and counting house in front; one large and one small parlor back, a delightful entry from the street to the yard. Upstairs is a good drawing room and three large chambers, with the same size cool passage, and in the best sitting room is Johnny's picture, which is an excellent likeness. After breakfast I hastily prepared to receive company which came in such numbers that I should have been quite tired out did not one frequently make their appearance whom I had before seen.

⚬∞⚬

Ann Warder was the daughter of English Quakers who lived in Ipswich, Suffolk. In her late twenties, she was visiting America for the first time. Her American husband, John Warder, also a Quaker, had come from Philadelphia to England a decade ago, on business, and had stayed on. Married for several years, they had three children, though only the eldest son, Jeremiah, came with them on this trip. They had left England in late April, and sailed to New York.

On this very last leg of a long journey, Ann Warder had come on ahead, to meet her in-laws for the first time: John's mother and a long train of older and younger relations. Reaching the house, she hurried through the door, presumably opened by a servant, before anybody noticed. She was now in the room with them. How would she be received?

The main reason for their journey to America was a dispute in John's family over his father's will. But if she had any doubts about her reception, they were immediately dispelled by such a welcome that "it would not be in my power to do justice to all the joy and affection shown me." It was like the sun coming out in a burst of warmth, the hints of cloud and mist melting away in its glow. She was happy because she was happily received: so happiness passes between people and they create the feeling for each other.

Then she watched as her husband arrived and was received with still deeper joy by her mother-in-law. She understood the older woman's "delight to see one who was always the darling, after ten years absence." The young Englishwoman was warmed by a double glow: first her own acceptance by the American in-laws, and then the warmth of this moment of deep restoration between mother and son. She was as joyful this time as witness as she had been "one hour and a half before" when she had been the central character.

A sense of belonging and peace filled Ann Warder's next morning, as she woke up to her new surroundings. She had "rested well in mother's best bed, the room large and house spacious." Everything was fine, bright, and airy. The outer world reflected her state of mind.

Two years later, she would in fact move her family to Philadelphia, never to return to England.

Leisure

The Amazing Pelican

John Evelyn, writer and scientist, writing in his diary

LONDON · FEBRUARY 9, 1665

I went to St. James's Park, where I saw various animals, and examined the throat of the Onocrotylus, or pelican, a fowl between a stork and a swan; a melancholy waterfowl, brought from Astrakhan by the Russian Ambassador; it was diverting to see how he would toss up and turn a flat fish, plaice, or flounder, to get it right into its gullet at its lower beak, which, being filmy, stretches to a prodigious wideness when it devours a great fish. Here was also a small waterfowl, not bigger than a moorhen, that went almost quite erect, like the penguin of America; it would eat as much fish as its whole body weighed; I never saw so insatiable a devourer, yet the body did not appear to swell the bigger. The Solan geese here are also great devourers, and are said soon to exhaust all the fish in a pond. Here was a curious sort of poultry not much exceeding the size of a tame pigeon, with legs so short as their crops seemed to touch the earth; a milk-white raven; a stork, which was a rarity at this season, seeing he was loose, and could fly loftily [. . .] The park was at this time stored with numerous flocks of several sorts of ordinary and extraordinary wild fowl, breeding about the Decoy, which for being near so great a city, and among such a concourse of soldiers and people, is a singular and diverting thing [. . .] There were withy-pots, or nests, for the wild fowl to lay their eggs in, a little above the surface of the water.

John Evelyn was in his mid-forties when he spent a clement winter day in London's first Royal Park. St. James's Park had recently been landscaped by King Charles II, who also opened it to the public. The king himself frequently went there, to feed the birds. It was as much an early zoological garden as a place of recreation. Evelyn was a passionate observer of both animal and plant life who wrote many books, including pioneering works about forest trees, natural history, and gardening. These interests were an important part of this wonderful February outing.

Evelyn partially went to the park to look at the various birds. It was a pelican that first caught his attention, a gift from Russia to the restored English king (Charles II had returned from exile in 1660). Evelyn loved the pelican, as children still do today in zoos around the world. He found it "diverting to see" how the bird maneuvered a big fish into its beak, and loved the pouch's "prodigious wideness." He felt real pleasure at being in the presence of something so ingenious, rare, and picturesque. It was the detail that entranced him.

From there, being now in an appreciative mood, he went on to admire another water bird that seemed even more impressive an eater of fish: "I never saw so insatiable a devourer." He was expecting the bird to become bloated with all the fish it consumed, and was amazed when it remained the same little bird.

After such sights, everything in this garden of curiosities pleased him. He relished every little detail of these creatures: short legs and milk-white feathers, tameness and appetite, as well as the hubbub of the breeding flocks. All of these small pleasures merged into one sensation of happiness when he thought that this entire park was "near so great a city, and among such a concourse of soldiers and people." The large and the small were beautifully bound together in a genuine appreciation of the natural world, brought to a capital of the human world.

The Count's Invitation to a Ball

Mary Wortley Montagu, author and traveler,
writing a letter to a friend

VIENNA · JANUARY 2, 1717

*One of the most accomplished men I have seen at Vienna is the young Count
Tarrocco, who accompanies the amiable Prince of Portugal. I am almost in love
with them both, and wonder to see such elegant manners, and such free and
generous sentiments in two young men that have hitherto seen nothing but
their own country. The Count [. . .] succeeds greatly with the devout beauties
here; his first overtures in gallantry are disguised under the luscious strains of
spiritual love [. . .]*

*Count Tarrocco is just come in—He is the only person I have excepted this
morning in my general order to receive no company—I think I see you smile—
but I am not so far gone as to stand in need of absolution; tho' as the human
heart is deceitful, and the Count very agreeable, you may think that even tho'
I should not want an absolution, I would nevertheless be glad to have an indulgence—No such thing—However, as I am a heretic, and you no confessor, I shall
make no declarations on this head—The design [purpose] of the Count's visit is
a ball—more pleasure—I shall be surfeited.*

Lady Mary Wortley Montagu, the wife of the courtier and diplomat Edward Wortley Montagu, had been one of the beauties and
sparkling wits of the British court after their marriage in 1712. She
counted among her friends many of the foremost writers of the time,
including the poet Alexander Pope and the dramatist John Gay.

In August 1716, she and Edward set off together to travel to Constantinople, where he had been appointed the British ambassador. She
had survived a serious smallpox infection two years previously. It had
left its mark, and she now needed all her courage and willpower to
plunge back into the sort of social life she had previously cherished.
She wrote home to her sister and to her literary friends, describing
her travels. This particular account was sent to the Abbé Antonio
Conti, a Catholic priest who was a distinguished natural philosopher

and mathematician and a member of the British Royal Society. She shared with Conti, a man with a more flexible ethical code than might have been expected, an intimate moment from her time in the Austrian capital.

In Vienna, the young Count Tarrocco appealed to her; she appreciated his charm and freshness. She also liked the prince, his companion. As a woman of the world, a veteran of London high life, she was intrigued by their sophistication, since in her view their background was a bit provincial. All of this was fascinating. It was like being inside a novel.

Then the novel came to life as she was writing to the abbé. The young count appeared in her apartments, with a heroic flourish. She was flustered. Her poise was shaken, and for a moment she felt a flush of the recent anxiety but also excitement, the thrill of intrigue and desire: "Count Tarrocco is just come in." So he was interested in her—that was a boost to her self-esteem and confidence.

The count departed, and she continued her letter in slightly coded terms to her confidant, playing with his power as a priest to grant absolution to the confessed sins of his flock. She almost made a confession. But then she just held back—teasing him with the idea of her being in need of an indulgence, and at the same time playing with the other meaning of indulgence.

The slightly frantic word play was part of her state of mind. Then she revealed the real cause of her excitement: the count had asked her to a ball. It was his "design," as she put it. Playfully she made the encounter sound full of intrigue and even danger.

The happiness of it all burst into bloom that she noted down quickly in the exclamation, "more pleasure." Then she hinted at further drama to follow, in a mocking parody of world-weary experience: "I shall be surfeited." Everything was exciting. She was truly alive in that moment.

The Governor's Guests

Ouyang Xiu, poet and provincial governor, composing a poetic essay

CHUZHOU, CHINA · CA. 1045

A cast in the stream, and a fine fish taken from some spot where the eddying pools begin to deepen; a draught of cool wine from the fountain; and a few such dishes of meats and fruits as the hills are able to provide; these, nicely spread out beforehand, constitute the Governor's feast. And in the revelry of the banquet hour there is no thought of toil or trouble. Every archer hits his mark, and every player wins his prize; goblets flash from hand to hand, and a buzz of conversation is heard as the guests move unconstrainedly about. Among them is an old man with white hair, bald at the top of his head. This is the drunken Governor who, when the evening sun kisses the tips of the hills and the falling shadows are drawn out and blurred, bends his steps homewards in company with his friends. Then in the growing darkness are heard sounds above and sounds below: the beasts of the field and the birds of the air are rejoicing at the departure of man. They, too, can rejoice in hills and in trees, but they cannot rejoice as man rejoices. So also the Governor's friends. They rejoice with him, though they know not at what it is that he rejoices. Drunk, he can rejoice with them; sober, he can discourse with them; such is the Governor. And should you ask who is the Governor, I reply, "Ouyang Xiu of Lu-ling."

Ouyang Xiu was the outstanding scholar and writer of his generation in China, and his work continued to be revered long after his death. He also had a controversial career in politics and administration. This particular passage comes from a brief poetic essay called "The Old Drunkard's Pavilion" that he wrote while he was exiled from court and installed as a governor in Anhui province. He was around forty, and his demotion from court occurred in a conflict between different factions over attempted reforms. But even his enemies, who were many, agreed that Ouyang Xiu was the supreme author of the day. Later, he was recalled to the capital and was given control of the entire civil service examination system.

But this passage is not about power or disappointment, rivalry or ambition during the Sung dynasty. Instead, Ouyang Xiu wrote about a traditional wooden pavilion in the countryside that he used for his own entertainments.

He began by telling the story of this pavilion, which had been erected by a Buddhist monk called Deathless Wisdom. It was already known locally because of the antics of a previous governor who visited there and frequently took too much wine. In the course of the essay, though, this previous governor was replaced by Ouyang Xiu himself as the drunken governor in the pavilion. This gives a fine shape to the vivid little picture of the occasion of his own "Governor's feast."

He described particular sounds and sights. A fishing line was cast in the river and a fish was caught. There was such peace that this little moment stood out clearly, as if it was the only important thing happening in the whole world.

The meal was fresh and local, and the wine was cool. There was no display and no competition. Even the games were devoid of real rivalry or strain. Everybody took the prize and the conversation also was open to all, easy and natural.

Ouyang Xiu loved the way people came together, making a kind of music out of their different voices. He was happy creating this moment in a small corner of the vast empire, under the shadow of the mountains. It hinted at how a good society might develop if fostered by such care and calm. Out of ordinary happiness and carefree community, another possible society, a different way of life, could be formed.

As the evening came, other sounds drifted into the pavilion, sounds of the birds and animals reclaiming their world. The human beings were leaving. Nature, too, was happy.

But his own satisfaction was something deeper, thought the drunken governor, as he enjoyed his friends' company. He felt a double happiness—he knew that he had entertained his guests well, just as he himself had enjoyed the conversations and the wine.

On Top of an Active Volcano

Mary Berry, author, writing in her travel journal

NAPLES · FEBRUARY 25, 1784

Set out at 8.30 a.m. for Vesuvius, with Mr. Musgrave, Mr. Coussmaker, and Mr. Clerk [. . .]

Arrived at the top [of Vesuvius], we were most amply repaid for any trouble the ascent had cost. We were two hours at the edge of the crater. During the whole of that time it threw up red-hot stones and scoriae [chunks of lava], and the wind for the most part blowing the smoke the other way, we saw continual volumes of flame, and looked quite down to the mouth of the crater. The surface of the present cone of Vesuvius is entirely the production of the last eruption: it is full of large cracks, out of all of which issues continued smoke. We crossed several of them in walking round the edge of the crater to that part where the last eruption broke through.

We dined upon the very edge of the crater, where we could look down into the fiery gulf and enjoy the noble fireworks with which it continued to treat us. The smoke which the wind every now and then brought over to our side was so full of sand that it much incommoded our eyes, and was so impregnated with sulphur that it made us all cough.

I descended from the crater to where our mules awaited us on foot, in, I believe, half an hour's time. The descent is most rapid, but, as the material on which one treads is soft, with the help of a stick or taking hold of an arm, one can jump forward without much fatigue.

❧

Mary Berry was born in 1763 in Yorkshire. A year later arrived her sister, Agnes, with whom she was always very close. Their mother died not long after, and the sisters were brought up by their father and grandmother, first in Yorkshire and then in London.

In May 1783, their father, Robert, a wealthy merchant, took the two young women with him on a long tour of Europe, through Holland and Belgium, then along the Rhine. By February 25, 1784, they were in southern Italy, about to climb the volcano Vesuvius outside Naples.

Italy was a favorite destination for many such Grand Tour travelers, and Mount Vesuvius was one of the regular places to visit there. The idea of ladies taking such rough and risky journeys, however, was rather new. But Mary Berry was no demure and passive gentlewoman. She was someone who saw the world in her own independent way. She was also a writer already, and as they passed the sites at the foot of the volcano, she was storing the images away for her travel journal. She was not so impressed by the ruins of Roman Herculaneum, destroyed in the great eruption of Vesuvius in 79 CE that had also buried Pompeii. "It is all buried seventy-five feet in a solid body of tufa [volcanic ash]," she wrote. The excavations had only begun in the 1700s, and in her view, it was all rather messy.

The English sisters were each carried in a chair by four locals as they got higher. Then they walked the last part. Mary Berry relished the effort and freedom, and then there was the wonderful moment when they reached the summit. It had only been a few years since the last big eruption, and Vesuvius was extremely active throughout the last decades of the eighteenth century. Nothing deterred the two sisters, not even the fact that "the whole of that time it threw up red-hot stones." A dangerous place.

But this was exactly where Mary Berry experienced a moment of most intense happiness. The views of Naples and its surroundings from the summit were grand. They went "walking round the edge" of the crater, and then they "dined upon the very edge" of it—a perfect spot, because they "could look down the fiery gulf." She felt she was in the audience for a personal performance of "the noble fireworks with which it continued to treat us." On top of it there was the pleasure of dining with such a spectacular view. Perfect bliss.

A Visit to a Literary Salon

Karl August Varnhagen von Ense, diplomat and author, writing in his journal

BERLIN · JULY 1806

The company [at Rahel Levin's salon] was extremely lively; each one with all ease and freedom contributed his part; artifice or hypocrisy had no chance of success. The unconstrained cheerfulness of Rahel, her spirit of truth and straightforwardness, reigned supreme. I was permitted with youthful extravagance to excite myself against the French; another to air his theatrical information; the Frenchman received facetious advice concerning his love affairs; while Schack [army officer] himself listened to the democratic outpourings of Vetter.

All went smoothly on; undue seriousness was lightened by wit and pleasantry, which in its turn was followed by sensible conversation, and so all was well balanced and full of animation. The open pianoforte invited to an occasional strain of music—Rahel herself being an accomplished and enthusiastic mistress of the art—and thus perfected the whole. We separated in good time in a mood of elevated thought, which I indulged for some time, out alone in the starlight, while I vainly scanned my past life for the memory of such another evening. My impatience would only allow a few days to elapse before repeating my visit.

⸎

Karl August Varnhagen von Ense was twenty-one and a serious young man. He was in Berlin officially to study medicine at the university, but he was spending most of his time reading literature and enjoying the cultural life of the city. That was why he had come to Rahel Levin's salon, for it was one of the most famous literary circles of its time. Here he was hoping to meet writers and poets, musicians and artists. He was not disappointed—but what impressed him even more was the hostess herself.

Levin was in her thirties, a German-Jewish woman from a comfortable background on the edges of the aristocratic circles. She had created this salon as her contribution to the cultural life of the time. In fact, this was its final year, since she was about to leave Berlin for

Paris. Although he did not realize it, the young man was witnessing an intellectual and artistic world that would soon lose its momentum.

He loved everything about the salon that July evening. Though he was probably younger than most of the other guests, and also less knowledgeable and experienced, they allowed him to have his own say, without making him feel ridiculous. He let off steam about the French—these were the years of the Napoleonic Wars—just as others had their opening to talk about whatever concerned them. This was a precious public-private space where people were free to speak as they wished.

The conversation was like an art form: harmonious and spontaneous, full of wit and yet with serious contributions as well. It was like a communal work of literature written in the air, just for that evening. These were people improvising on themes of which they never tired, in which they always found more depth and beauty. It was talk as art, but shared and tolerant rather than a matter of display or competition.

Then Varnhagen von Ense noticed his hostess properly. Her cameo on the piano brought the occasion to its light and fitting climax. It was as if the conversation had been turned into a melody. The whole evening seemed to reflect and express Rahel Levin's personality. (Some years later, in fact, they married each other.)

He went out and looked at the sky. The stars above Berlin seemed brighter this night. Even the heavens were in tune with this deeply harmonious evening. Thinking over the happiest moments in his life so far, he could find nothing to beat it. Life had shown him the best it had to offer.

A Doorway into Antiquity

Benjamin Silliman, scientist, writing in his journal

LONDON · JUNE 12, 1805

In the yard before the [British] Museum, beneath temporary sheds [. . .] till they can be removed into a building now erecting for their reception, are the celebrated antiques, taken from General Menou at Alexandria [. . .] Among them are several Roman statues [. . .] an ancient obelisk and several images, supposed to have been intended to represent the Egyptian goddess Isis; but a number of sarcophagi are justly reckoned among the greatest curiosities [. . .]

The largest and most ornamented of these sarcophagi is believed to have been the exterior coffin in which the body of Alexander the Great was deposited. Giving way to the impression which I strongly felt to believe the fact, I was forcibly struck with the humiliating lesson which it reads to human ambition, and especially to the thirst for martial glory [. . .]

With similar emotions I beheld a collection of arms found on the place where the great battle of Cannae [Carthage against Rome, in 216 BCE] was fought, and supposed to have belonged to the parties who contended on that memorable spot. There is also a collection of rings and of other ornaments for the fingers and ears, which are believed to have been worn by the combatants at Cannae. In spite of the disposition which is so naturally felt to ridicule an enthusiastic and extravagant admiration of antiquity, one cannot remain unaffected when he realizes that these rings have been worn on Roman fingers; this helmet covered a Carthaginian head; and that spear was thrown by a Roman hand in the presence of the victorious Hannibal. Similar emotions were excited by the numerous Roman vases; the amphorae in which their wines were kept; and especially by the relics of the unfortunate Herculaneum. These consist of utensils, vases, gods, etc., and among other things are the very hinges of their doors. By the sight of these authentic remnants of this illustrious nation, a powerful impulse is excited towards the study of their antiquities.

～≫

Benjamin Silliman was twenty-five when he came to Britain to further his education. He had been a law tutor at Yale University (his alma mater), but Yale's president at the time, Timothy Dwight, wanted him to requalify to teach science. Silliman first studied science in Philadelphia, and then sought out scientists in England and Scotland. He did, on returning to Yale, teach chemistry, helped found Yale Medical School, and launched the *American Journal of Science*.

On this June day, he visited the British Museum in London. The museum was then half a century old, but its collection had just grown as a result of many valuable objects—particularly Egyptian mummies—acquired by the British after the surrender of the French general Menou at Alexandria in 1801. Rebuilding was going on to add exhibition space, and so the treasures were stored in makeshift sheds, "constructed to defend them from the weather, till they can be removed into a building."

Benjamin Silliman cast a detached eye over the sarcophagi. But gradually, something began to stir in him. He thought first of Alexander the Great (this was not, in fact, his coffin), and then he began to imagine the soldiers who had carried these weapons and worn these rings and helmets during the Battle of Cannae. He looked at the rings and ornaments, reflecting how "one cannot remain unaffected when he realizes that these rings have been worn on Roman fingers." They must have been prized possessions. And he could feel what it was like to have the weight of a helmet on one's head, or a spear in one's hand.

His sense of excitement deepened. He loved the small things, like the vases and amphorae, and "the very hinges of their doors" from tragic Herculaneum. What had seemed mere objects now came to life in his imagination, things that people had handled in centuries long past. He was not looking only with his head but also with his heart, and so "emotions were excited by the numerous Roman vases," and he was happy to be in the presence of the amphorae because these were the very jars "in which their wines were kept." He felt a burst of joy at sensing the sheer life of the past.

The Landscape Painting

Emma Willard, educator, writing a letter to her sister

PARIS · DECEMBER 18, 1830

When I tell you that I devoted this morning to viewing the pictures in the gallery of the Louvre, you will probably expect me to come out in quite a rhapsody, as you know my great fondness for paintings. I was indeed quite rapt, as I walked slowly up the long gallery, and got into the spirit of the different feelings, which the whole scene is calculated to inspire: admiration—loathing—pity—disgust—veneration—and the spirit of laughter [. . .]—and besides this, the spirit of severe reprehension; all these feelings rose by turns, or mingled together in my mind [. . .] Yet I dare say, I shall go often to the gallery, but I shall learn to do by these pictures, as I do by Paris generally [. . .] I control my eyes, and my mind; and look at what I like, and pass over the rest as if it were not.

There are two comparatively small apartments [in the Louvre], filled with paintings before you enter the grand gallery. Among these my attention was particularly fixed by one landscape. It had, upon the grass and shrubs which skirted its living waters, the fresh dew of morning when the sun's first rays give to it its sparkling brightness.

⟨✦⟩

Emma Willard was a pioneer of women's education in America. After founding an academy for young women in Middlebury, Vermont, she started the Troy Female Seminary in upstate New York in 1821. Its curriculum was revolutionary at the time, offering young women a varied education with a distinctive emphasis on self-expression and the attainment equal to that of male students. Willard's approach was distinctive, with a strong emphasis on culture and creativity unusual at a time when rote learning was more common.

In 1830, she was in her forties. She had lost her husband five years ago, and now she was coming to Europe to meet other educators and see the great museums. She arrived at the famous Louvre thinking of herself as someone who loved art, and she remarked to her sister, "you will probably expect me to come out in quite a rhapsody." She expected this herself. She was certainly gripped when she looked around the great collection: "I was indeed quite rapt, as I walked slowly up the long gallery."

But she was awash with a tide of conflicting emotions. She disliked the mixture of sacred and secular images, she was appalled by some of the paintings, and others struck her as absurd. She decided to learn to practice selective viewing.

Then her gaze settled on one painting, in a smaller room of the Louvre. "My attention was particularly fixed by one landscape." By "landscape" she meant both a genre of painting and also the view itself. Stillness came over Emma Willard as she entered this painted world of a quiet dawn.

She forgot about her surroundings, her moral judgments, and simply let her imagination loose. Details of the landscape came to life when she noticed "upon the grass and shrubs which skirted its living waters, the fresh dew of morning." She felt the sun rising and the rays giving to the scene "its sparkling brightness." Delayed by indignation and distraction, her happiness was all the greater when it came. The "waters" in the painting were "living" for her because of their illusion of movement. They also felt like a spiritual current, carrying energy and renewal into the heart of the rapt viewer.

This private happiness in a moment of leisure contributed to her educational vision of introducing young women to "that art, which obliges us to study Nature, in order to imitate her [and] often enkindles the latent spark of taste—of sensibility for her beauties, till it glows to adoration for their Author, and a refined love of all His works." She had gone beyond the kind of technical appreciation that would have been the educational orthodoxy of her time. This was the artistic vision that she wanted to share with her female students.

Magic Lights and Fireworks
under the Moon

Jane Knox, belated honeymooner, writing in her diary

ROME · APRIL 11, 1819

Went to see High Mass performed at St. Peter's [Basilica], but were unable to stay all the time. But we saw the Pope give the Benediction from the front window, and he threw down two indulgences. This sight was an impressive one, the crowd being immense. In the evening we went to see St. Peter's illuminated. We took up a position in our carriages. At first the partial illumination was not striking, but at eight o'clock the change took place almost instantaneously to a scene of the most dazzling brilliancy. It was done by machinery most ingeniously contrived by Michelangelo. Each lamp had been covered with oiled paper; this is removed, and the torches placed between are suddenly lighted. Directly after we had seen this we moved towards the Castle of San Angelo, but the crowd was so great that we could not reach it till near ten, when we got to a window and saw the fireworks of the Castle. They were more magnificent than I can describe; impossible to imagine anything more beautiful. We next walked to the Trinita dei Monti [Renaissance church] to see the illumination from that height. The moonlight was bright, but it did not spoil the effect in the least.

⁂

Jane Knox was from a Scottish aristocratic family. Her husband, Edmond Knox, was the second son of aristocratic parents. Born Jane Sophia Hope-Vere in around 1790, she had experienced a difficult childhood despite her privileged background, since she was sent by her parents to be cared for by strangers who treated her harshly. When she encountered Edmond on a visit to London, she was soon won over by the young naval officer, recording on June 13, 1813: "I had an interview with Captain Knox before church. Engaged myself to him." They married the same year, but due to his seafaring career, it was only in the autumn of 1818 that they embarked together on their extended "honeymoon" tour of the continent.

This April evening in 1819 comes from their travels in Italy. To begin with, the Knoxes were in rather a hurry. They were "unable to stay" for the whole of high mass at St. Peter's. It was perhaps longer than they anticipated.

When evening fell, they returned to St. Peter's, to see it illuminated. Their carriage was carefully parked to give the right view. But to start with, Jane Knox was surprised and disappointed at "the partial illumination." They had come to see the magnificent lights. They expected something grand, but instead it all seemed rather dim and ordinary.

Eight o'clock struck. In an instant, the basilica burst into light, shining with "the most dazzling brilliancy." That transformation brought about an equally instant change in her mood. Suddenly, the world was lit up, inside and out. Instead of being rushed and dissatisfied, prepared for potential disappointment, she was entranced.

Then, already happy, the couple set off to find a different spectacle—the fireworks at Castel Sant'Angelo. Once again, a note of complaint returned when people got in their way and "the crowd was so great that we could not reach it till near ten." Eventually, Jane Knox found a good spot from which to see the promised fireworks, "more magnificent" than she had words to express. A world that so often fell below her expectations had for once surpassed them.

The couple then walked to the church Trinità dei Monti, atop the Spanish Steps. From here they could see the city lights below and also the moonlight up above. The shadow of a complaint passed through her mind as she wondered if the moonlight might "spoil the effect," but it did not do so "in the least" on that happy evening.

After her uneasy childhood and the years of separation from her seafaring husband, Jane Knox was at peace, able to enjoy the sights and sounds of the great city on an evening of companionable exploration.

Nature

The Bliss of Skating

George Head, army officer and explorer, writing in his travel journal

PENETANGUISHENE, ONTARIO · MARCH 6, 1815

In the morning the aspect of the country was altogether and totally changed. The snow was covered with a glassy coating of ice, and the whole of the bay was nearly frozen over. The pools of clear water the day before had been so large and numerous [. . .] and as there had been no wind in the night, the ice upon them was clear and good. Instead of my moccasins, I put on a pair of shoes, to which I had been for a long time unused, and going down to the bay, sat down upon a large stone to put on my skates. It was a lovely morning; the sun shone quite bright, while the frost was remarkably keen; and in a very few minutes I was carried rapidly along towards the opposite shore. The glow of exercise, the lively rattle of the skates, and the sensation produced by the fresh air, combined to embellish the novelty of the scene before me, as I ranged with unlimited freedom [over] the clear ice which extended all across the bay. Every object around me was unexplored, while I had the means of being conveyed, as it were on wings, from one to the other. I had been confined for many weeks, either sitting still half frozen in a carriage the whole of the day, or, since my arrival in the forest, completely weather-bound. For a long period I had never been thoroughly warm, only barely able to subdue cold, and had seldom during the whole day felt a dry stocking on my foot.

My blood was now in full circulation, and the interest I felt in every thing around me was so great, that the sun had nearly reached the tops of the trees before I thought of returning to my dwelling.

❧

George Head was in his thirties, a British army officer who had served under General Wellington in the Peninsular War against Napoleon. He had been promoted to assistant commissary general in 1814 and put in charge of supplies for Wellington's Third Army in Spain. Then, in October 1814, he was sent to Halifax, Nova Scotia, where he arrived in late November. The "passage of the river St. Lawrence being already closed for the winter," he journeyed overland to wintry Quebec and York (Toronto). His destination was the small settlement of Penetanguishene, on Georgian Bay, "where it was the object of Government to establish a naval and military post."

On February 28, 1815, he and his party "came upon Gloucester Bay, and from there we reached that of Penetanguishene." It was a day of satisfaction and relief: "Here, then, I was arrived!" They had covered many miles in one day's travel across the icy land. But the relief soon gave way to further discomfort: "On stepping out of the sleigh I was immediately wet through, owing to sinking half way up my legs in melted snow." They came to a cluster of cabins where he began, over the following days, the construction of his own cabin. He worked hard with an axe cutting down the trees himself alongside the workmen.

Having spent the preceding days in such toil, George Head awoke on March 6 to find the world transfigured by "a glassy coating of ice." Sensing the special quality of this day, he took a break from his labors and, "going down to the bay, sat down upon a large stone" in order to put on his skates. Appreciation for the unique atmosphere of that "lovely morning" filled his journal entry. He set off skating across the ice where all sense of effort fell from him, as "in a very few minutes I was carried rapidly along," making for the far shore. Liberated for a short while from his military duties, he could enjoy "the glow of exercise." Small things made an intense impression, like the rattling of the skates. The conscientious officer felt for an interval the pure joy of "unlimited freedom."

An Amusing Owl

Gilbert White, curate and naturalist, writing in his diary

SELBORNE, HAMPSHIRE · AUGUST 27, 1791

A fern owl this evening showed off in a very unusual and entertaining manner, by hawking round and round the circumference of my great spreading oak for twenty times following, keeping mostly close to the grass, but occasionally glancing up amidst the boughs of the tree. This amusing bird was then in pursuit of a brood of some particular Phalaena [moths] belonging to the oak, of which there are several sorts; and exhibited on the occasion a command of wing superior, I think, to that of the swallow itself.

When a person approaches the haunt of fern owls in an evening, they continue flying round the head of the obtruder; and by striking their wings together above their backs, in the manner that the pigeons called smiters are known to do, make a smart snap: perhaps at that time they are jealous for their young; and this noise and gesture are intended by way of menace.

Fern owls have attachment to oaks, no doubt on account of food; for the next evening we saw one again several times among the boughs of the same tree; but it did not skim round its stem over the grass, as on the evening before. In May these birds find the Scarabeus Melolontha [scarab beetle] on the oak; and the Scarabeus Solstitialis [scarab beetle] at midsummer. These peculiar birds can only be watched and observed for two hours in the twenty-four; and then in a dubious twilight an hour after sunset and an hour before sunrise.

⌐∞⌐

Gilbert White was the curate of Selborne, a village in southern England. In earlier years, he had been a fellow of Oriel College, Oxford University, and a curate in several parishes. Now he was an elderly man who had lived in one place for three decades. He was a notable amateur naturalist, recording for many years the birds and other wildlife of his area. Although his book, *The Natural History and Antiquities of Selborne*, later became a celebrated classic of nature writing, it is in his vast personal diary that he left a most original and complete record of the day-to-day changes in the world around him.

On this August evening in 1791, the light was fading. This was a good time of day for him because he loved, above all things, to watch the birds on the trees, in the fields, and hedges of the countryside he had come to know so well. He had been keeping a careful record of the comings and goings of different species.

This evening he strolled down toward a favorite tree, "my great spreading oak," that stood in his field at a distance from his house. There he noticed the owl. Expertly, he recognized the species—a fern owl. He knew all about them and their habits, like the way they swooped on intruders.

But he was not interested only in classifying various birds. He even recognized individuals and their personalities, like the "amusing bird" he encountered on this summer evening. He found character in this particular owl, without humanizing it or forgetting its true nature.

He stood quiet and watched as the bird went "hawking round and round," encircling the trunk of the great oak as if it had been enchanted, staying mostly close to the ground, then suddenly dipping up.

Gilbert White was mesmerized. He also understood the intentions behind this entertaining performance. There were moths living in this tree, a good evening meal for the owl.

His moment of happiness was a perfect balance between knowledge and imagination, understanding and admiration as the owl "exhibited on the occasion a command of wing superior [. . .] to that of the swallow itself." He was especially moved because fern owls could "only be watched and observed for two hours in the twenty-four." It was a precious gift from this departing day.

His whole personality was engaged, he was enjoying everything about the owl's existence here in this field. Without trying to take possession of the owl in any way, he felt a connection with it, and he loved it for its freedom and enjoyment of flying.

A Vast Sheet of Frozen Water

William Whewell, scientist and philosopher,
writing a letter to a friend

VALAIS, SWITZERLAND · AUGUST 18, 1829

From the sight of the Rhône glacier [canton of Valais, Switzerland] [. . .] I have learnt that nature has a love for the form of a waterfall such as I desired to see, but that for some good reason (possibly to prevent the valley below from being inundated) she turned the waterfall to ice as soon as she had set it a-going. You are to imagine [. . .] a waterfall half-a-mile broad and a thousand feet high, leaping down between mountains, gigantic even when compared with its dimensions, and laden with eternal snows; and you are to suppose that this vast sheet of water, as soon as it touches the bottom of the valley into which it plunges, boils up and spreads itself over a far wider space as it rushes away. You are then to wave the wand of your imagination a second time, and to turn all this cataract to ice, and you will have the glacier of the Rhône. You are to suppose all the partial torrents and bounds of water which are woven together to make its expanse to be modelled in strange and fantastic pyramids of ice with deep blue chasms between [. . .] To look it in the face under a beautiful blue sky is a good employment for an August morning.

⌀

William Whewell was born in Lancaster, England, in 1794, as son of a carpenter. In 1811, he won a scholarship to Trinity College, Cambridge University. After a distinguished undergraduate performance, he became a college fellow in 1817. He was talented in many fields, especially in mathematics, and became a friend of other leading mathematical figures such as Charles Babbage, the inventor of a first prototype of the computer. A prolific and wide-ranging author, Whewell's earliest books were on physics and geology; in 1828, the year preceding this visit to the Swiss Alps, he had become professor of mineralogy at Cambridge.

Whewell had set off for his Continental summer tour on July 4, 1829, going first to Cologne and Darmstadt in Germany. He enjoyed discussions with scientific colleagues and visiting the tourist sites, such as Cologne Cathedral.

Then there was his mountain adventure. He recorded "walking twenty or thirty miles a day among the highest parts of the Alps," and one of these days he "arrived at the glacier from which the Rhône issues." He was excited both as a geologist and as a tourist.

He had been eager to see waterfalls, he confided in this letter to his friend Hugh Rose, a clergyman, and now he was granted that wish, though in an unexpected way. Looking at the immense glacier, he imagined it as a torrent of Alpine water that had been turned into ice, preventing the valley below from becoming flooded.

As a geologist, Whewell was interested in the ways in which the current landscape had come into existence. He saw the present scene as an expression of distant causes; but this was a friendly and informal letter, so instead of presenting a theory of glacial formation, he called on his friend to wave the wand of his imagination: first to summon up the fearsome prospect of a gigantic waterfall, then the magical transformation of all this water into ice and snow. There is a sense of wonder in his vivid words describing the "vast sheet of water" that, in its frozen state, "plunges, boils up and spreads itself" across the floor of the valley and creates "fantastic pyramids of ice."

Part of Whewell's point, though he left it implicit, was that the world had not always looked the way it did now. There had been eras, long ago, when the earth underwent immense changes. The science of geology had made considerable advances in the 1700s, and was now brought to vivid life with a flick of the writer's own magic wand of eloquent imagination. There is immense intellectual satisfaction behind his words, the pleasure of being in the presence of such unique evidence for the ideas that he was working on, ideas about the distant prehistory of the modern continents and their mountains, valleys, and rivers.

This was altogether a fine way to spend a summer day in the Swiss Alps, one of the most majestic landscapes and a great monument to the history of earth itself—a day filled with the joy of both taking in and understanding the natural world.

The First Sight of the Mountains

Lucy Larcom, teacher and poet, writing in her journal

MAINE · AUGUST 1860

It rained on the way, but it was only the cooler and more comfortable traveling for that; and when the sun came out in the west just as we reached the top of a ridge from which the whole long mountain chain was visible on the horizon, I felt that that one view was enough compensation for going, and that first glimpse I shall never forget. The round summit of [Mount] Blue, and the bolder ridges of Saddleback and Abraham [mountains], lifted themselves above the lower elevations that would be mountains anywhere but among mountains, far off and solemn with the deepening purple of sunset, and over them the sky hung, fiery gold, intermingled with shadow. The first glimpse was finer than anything afterward, though I rode up the lovely valley of the Sandy River, which is like a paradise, if not one, recalling ever the old words of the hymn: "Sweet fields arrayed in living green, / And rivers of delight."

❦

Lucy Larcom was thirty-six in the summer of 1860. In her childhood, following the death of her father, she had had to work in the mills in Lowell, Massachusetts. Her talent as a child poet had attracted support, and she eventually obtained a teaching degree. For several years now, she had been a teacher at a seminary in her home state. She had also published a poem in a literary magazine that had received wide acclaim.

She had never seen these mountains of Maine before. When she had left Massachusetts before, in the 1840s, it had been to teach at a school in Illinois. Now her summer vacation from the seminary had taken her to these new scenes, and she loved the freshness of the experience.

That particular August day, on the way to the mountains, it rained, but it made the traveling easier. Late in the afternoon, the summer sun appeared just as she "reached the top of a ridge."

In that sudden sunshine, she glimpsed for the first time a "long mountain chain" in the distance. Though it was far away, the whole scene was "one view," burning a single image into her mind. At its center, there was the striking "round summit of Blue."

It all came together like a pattern of balanced opposites, round and edgy, high and low, light and dark. She was happy that a whole world had opened up instantaneously before her.

Lucy Larcom knew that her "first glimpse" of these mountains was bound to be "finer" than anything that would come afterwards—a glimpse she would "never forget." She returned to this thought a little later: "What can be more beautiful than green meadowlands, bordered by forest-covered slopes, that ever rise and rise, till they fade into dim blue mountain-distances?" Nevertheless, she did try the next day to re-create the original excitement and get closer to one of the summits itself: "I climbed one mountain halfway—the bluest of the blue—and so called, by emphasis, Mount Blue." But it wasn't quite the same, since "the distant view is always more impressive, more full of suggestions for me." On the final day of her vacation, as she passed that glorious viewpoint of the first evening, she "hoped for a repetition of the first delight. But the far-off ridges were closely veiled with mist and rain, and a thundershower swept toward us from them, across the wide valley."

But there was one final blessing: "Yet as we turned to leave, Mount Blue just lifted off his mist-cap for a few minutes, as if to say good-bye." She was now able to visualize the mountain from memory: "Altogether, it is a most charming and comforting picture for future remembrance: flowery mountain slopes, little garden patches of goldenrod, white everlasting and purple willow herb, under the shade of maples, and firs, and graceful hemlocks; and glimpses of cottagers' homes on hillsides and by running streams." The magic of the original moment was safely preserved, deep inside her: "My eyes are rested, and my heart is glad."

The Celebrated Pine Tree

Matsuo Basho, poet and traveler,
writing in his travel journal

TAKEKUMA, JAPAN · SUMMER OF 1689

My heart leaped up when I saw the pine tree at Takekuma. Its roots split out from the ground into two trunks, proof that it looks as it did in ancient times. My thoughts turned to the Abbot Noin [recluse and poet]. A long time ago, the newly appointed Governor of Mutsu Province had cut down this tree and used the wood as stakes to support the bridge over the River Natori. When Noin came here [nearly seven centuries before Basho], he wrote that no trace of the tree remained. I had heard that this tree had been felled time after time, generation after generation, only for a new tree to be grafted onto the stump each time. But now it seems to have attained the splendid power to last a thousand years—it is truly a wonderful sight.

⚬⚬⚬

In May of 1689, Matsuo Basho set off on a journey that would last nine months among the uplands and lowlands, the forests and the shores of Japan. In his mid-forties, he was already a famous poet, a leading practitioner of the art of haiku, the short, highly structured poem for which Japanese literature is now globally celebrated. Yet Basho had not come from a wealthy or powerful background. His brothers were farmers. He himself, son of a minor samurai, had been in the service of a local lord until the man's death had set him free. Then he had moved to the capital, Edo (Tokyo), where he taught and wrote poetry.

In 1684, he had made the first of several journeys that he recorded in unique travel journals, a personal blend of poetry and description. These journeys were becoming increasingly important in his life. He called them "wayfaring," as distinct from pilgrimages. He described himself as a kind of human bat, a cross between a bird and a mouse, between a monk and a secular man.

An early highlight of this journey in 1689 was his visit to see this long-famous pine tree. He had known about it, and now he was here.

He loved the way the real tree in front of his eyes resembled the one described in ancient texts, its single root dividing into two trunks.

As he stood there looking at the tree, feeling his heart leap up, his memory filled with human voices. There had been another poet, Abbot Noin, who had come to Takekuma only to find the tree "cut down," turned into supports for a bridge by an officious governor. After many generations and many new grafts, now the twin trunks were here again.

He also recalled a more recent voice, that of his friend Kyohaku, who had wished Basho well when he set off on the journey. In the form of a haiku, he had emphasized that Basho should see this pine tree at Takekuma. Now that wish was fulfilled. Basho acknowledged it in his reply to Kyohaku.

For Basho, the happiness of being in the presence of nature was common ground across the millennia. When he stood in front of a majestic pine tree like this one, he was in communion both with the natural world and with his human ancestors. Joy in nature was a thread connecting different lives. Indeed, this sense of interconnectedness was perhaps an essential part of the feeling itself.

The Wonderful Mist of the Waterfall

John Goldie, botanist, writing in his diary

NEAR LAKE ONTARIO, ONTARIO · JULY 8, 1819

The country through which I passed today was generally well settled and of rather good quality, but all inclining to sand. This day I crossed three consid-erable creeks which run very much below the level of the adjacent land; their banks are both high and very steep, so that it must have been with a good deal of difficulty that a road has been made across them. The road is mostly com-posed of wood which forms a barrier to the earth that is cut from the bank. After travelling about twenty-eight miles I came alongside the west corner of Lake Ontario, where the first object that I noticed was what appeared to me to be a great body of smoke on the opposite side of the lake; but you may guess my incredulous surprise and pleased astonishment when I was informed that that was the spray of the Great Falls. It appeared very distinctly and as if at no great distance; and in the calm mornings and evenings the sound of the Falls is distinctly heard at this place which is thirty miles distant in a direct line.

❧

John Goldie was in his late twenties when he had this extraordi-nary day near Niagara Falls. He had grown up in a small village in rural Ayrshire in Scotland. But instead of following his forebears into the old life of small farmers, he had trained as a botanist and gardener at the Glasgow Botanic Gardens. This won him sufficient support to finance the beginning of a trip to study the plants and geology of North America. He was ultimately successful and sent specimens to the famous collection first established by Sir Joseph Banks at Kew Gardens near London. But initially it had been some-thing of a struggle.

He had sailed for North America in June 1817. He landed at Hali-fax, Nova Scotia, and then made the journey to Quebec, where he began his botanical survey. For a while he taught at a school and now, in the summer of 1819, he was exploring along the route from Mon-treal to Pittsburgh. Here he had more success than before and found many rare plants.

It was still a difficult place as far as Goldie was concerned. He was now on the western shore of Lake Ontario. He had passed another "disagreeable night," plagued by mosquitoes and unhappy with the inn in general. Not only that, but when the day began he had all the troubles of the journey again. (He was walking, after all, and carrying a heavy load with his belongings and equipment.) He responded by being meticulous and carefully recording the land in scientific and botanical terms. Being practical, he noted that it was "inclining to sand" and that the deep creeks made it difficult to construct a good road. His mood subtly improved at this point. He was full of admiration for human willpower and ingenuity overcoming the hostile environment. He was a man with the future in his eyes.

But it was still so far only an "ordinary" botanist's day, until John Goldie suddenly noticed "a great body of smoke on the opposite side of the lake." Could there be a huge wildfire?

Then uncertainty gave way to "incredulous surprise and pleased astonishment"—these were the majestic Niagara Falls. He had begun the day quite lugubriously, and now he felt a rare upsurge of pleasure. In one moment he had left all the annoyances behind and entered instead a magic land where a cloud of smoke turned to mist and fire to water. He was glad to be there now.

The falls themselves remained hidden over the horizon. Only the cloud of mist revealed their power, and then he also became aware of their sound, like perpetual thunder. The wonder of things, the joy of nature, came not easy to him, a man who was usually sealed off from such reactions by a scientific calm. In future years, he was to travel as far as Russia on other botanical quests, but eventually he returned to western Ontario with his family to settle. The "Great Falls" had entranced him for life.

New Year's Day in the Heavens and on Earth

Hattori Ransetsu, courtier and poet, composing a haiku

KYOTO, JAPAN · CA. 1700

New Year's Day, ah yes!
With the skies clear
And sparrows' conversation.

⟨∞⟩

Around the year 1700 in Japan, Hattori Ransetsu was a leading poet of haiku, writing about places and trees, the changing sky and passing experiences. Though little is known of his life, it is documented that his work was admired by his renowned teacher, Basho.

Ransetsu wrote this haiku to record a Japanese New Year's Day. He was a man about fifty, and had in fact only a few more years to live. But in these words he expressed his positive feeling of the coming of another year. Since the days were slowly getting longer again, he was responding to the rebirth of the natural world as well as to an annual communal celebration of new beginnings.

First he recorded just the simplest fact of the day, the date in the calendar, official timing. It was a joyful day, as he had celebrated it many times before.

That was followed by an exclamation—"ah yes!"—which feels as if he was grasping the positive aura of this particular New Year's Day moment. This expression was as fundamental as could have been (a single syllable in Japanese): the purest possible affirmative mood as nature and humankind turned once more toward the next season.

He took stock of the feeling of the day and the world. He absorbed the reverberation of this basic and almost pure "yes" that seemed to be there all around him. Looking up, the sky was "clear." No clouds, nothing closing the horizon. There was only the open blue of the heavens and the first sunlight of the new year. The cloudless sky was another aspect of this overarching feeling of simplicity and purity. The sky was reduced to its core.

From the tall to the tiny: after the immense vista of the sky, Ransetsu's attention shifted to the small birds close at hand. They seemed to be rather like people, chattering among themselves in a "sparrows' conversation." It was as if they shared in the energy and the enthusiasm of the new year.

There were three parts to this moment for the poet: the huge silent sky, the small chatty sparrows, and he himself, aware of all three. Everything joined together in his observing mind and expressed for him the essence of this festive day.

It is said that Hattori Ransetsu became a Buddhist monk for the last years of his life, perhaps in response to the death of his teacher Basho. If this haiku was written around 1700, then Ransetsu would only enjoy a few more New Year's Day celebrations—he died in 1707. Here he achieved a clarity of vision that mirrored the clear light of the moment and became the perfect vehicle for a feeling of uncomplicated acceptance, of a happiness pure and simple that arises from the continuing existence of the living world through the cycles of the years and the generations.

On Top of the World

Edward Price, artist, writing in his travel journal

KONGSVOLD, NORWAY · SEPTEMBER 1826

I left Drivstuen early in the morning, and had a saddle-horse to Kongsvold [. . .] The road was for some miles very precipitous. Near Kongsvold the rocky bed of a river, deep, savage, and dark, was indicative of the grand scenery whence it has its source; the rocks were hoary with reindeer moss; and the fir, ever attendant on a Norway river, deepened the gloom of the valley. The country is very wild and rugged between Kongsvold and Jerkin, and the road uphill all the way, till within a short distance of the station. The morning was cloudless and frosty.

When I arrived at Jerkin, I requested that a guide might be ready after breakfast, to accompany me to the summit of Sneehaettan [Snøhetta]; this was immediately complied with, and he waited my pleasure with a pony, and two long sticks, which were to come into use when we reached the snow. It was about ten o' clock in the morning when we set off, and the distance to the highest point appeared so inconsiderable [short], that I thought to give an hurra on the top, and to return to Jerkin the same day. There was a freshness in the morning which was very exhilarating, and the delicate blue and white of the snow heights were a contrast to peat bogs and brown herbage which occupied the whole of the intervening space.

⌁∞⌁

Edward Price, born in 1801, was an English landscape artist. He had studied with the reputable landscape artist John Glover, and Glover included some of Price's works in his London exhibitions in 1823/24.

Now Price had had the idea of making small, illustrated books and had come to the picturesque mountainsides of Norway for a first attempt. (He followed this volume of views of Norway with others on the English Lake District and Peak District.) He also recorded how he felt on that particular day in Norway's Dovrefjell mountains, some two hundred miles north of Oslo.

He started this day's journey from an ancient mountain inn at Drivstuen and proceeded by way of other inns at Kongsvold and Jerkin. It was a steep and even dangerous road through wilderness, and he came to the banks of a "savage" river where even the rocks were "hoary with reindeer moss." The atmosphere was both menacing and magical, full of romantic allure for a traveler from rather urban and tame England. The morning sky was "cloudless and frosty."

Then there was breakfast in Jerkin, where he made arrangements for the climb up to the summit of Snøhetta. He needed a guide, who was waiting for him when the meal was done. He noted the pony "and two long sticks, which were to come into use when we reached the snow." It was all rather fascinating to him.

They set off at "about ten o'clock." He looked up toward the mountain peak. He knew that it would be a long climb. Then he had a simple, happy moment, which went beyond the ordinary enjoyment of the day. In the bright morning air, the snow-covered mountain seemed up close, "and the distance to the highest point appeared so inconsiderable." It was as if he could very soon "give an hurra on the top." He felt as if he could stretch out a hand and touch the summit of the mountain.

It would in fact take several hours to reach the summit that had seemed so close. Trudging through rough scrubland by the side of a river, Price and his guide eventually reached an altitude at which snow became thick and the air grew thinner. The experienced guide pleaded with the traveler to turn back, but the Englishman was not to be deterred. They gained the summit in the evening light and the view was very rewarding as "one illumined snow peak after another sunk into shadow." Yet the descent proved beyond Price's strength. He lay down and the guide had to light a fire and build a makeshift camp for the night. In the morning, Price learned that a wolf had been prowling nearby!

Yet that original moment before the ascent remained untarnished. Normally, Edward Price was methodical. He planned, observed, and recorded everything. But here, in the wilds of Norway, he experienced this burst of happiness as he pictured himself standing on top of the highest peak. For that magic moment of immediacy, there had been nothing at all between the young artist and the top of the world.

A Fine White Beach

Hannah Callender, young woman, writing in her diary

QUEENS, NEW YORK · APRIL 1759

*From thence went to the beach. The fine white sand along it is so hard that rid-
ing makes no impression on it. We rode several miles sometimes in the waves,
which seem to meet you as though they would overwhelm. There are beacons
placed on a hill to alarm the country in case of an invasion. We saw some ships
out at sea, which looks of a green cast. The hills of Shrewsbury [in New Jersey]
appeared at a vast distance. The riding is so fine that there are often great
wagers won by racing. We bade adieu to one of the most glorious sights my eyes
ever beheld and rode through a pleasant country to Jamaica [Queens County],
where we dined. After dinner the company was full of mirth. J. R. inquiring
how I liked the country, told me there was a place just by called Horsemanden's
folly or Mount Lookout, built round the body of a large tree to a great height,
ascended by winding stairs. At the top it is floored and there is a table, half a
dozen may drink tea on comfortably. I said I had a great desire to see it, and
run from this crazy company. We went to a [sedan] chair and got in. It soon
took wind where we were going, and the rest followed. Eighteen in so small a
place made some of them fearful. The prospect was as far as the ken of sight.
We saw the beach we had that morning been on.*

❧

Hannah Callender grew up in a well-off Quaker family. She was born
in 1737, in Philadelphia. Her grandparents had been Scottish Quakers
who had left the Old World to find a place less hostile to their faith.

But the previous years had been extremely difficult for the pacifist
Quakers of the American colonies. The so-called French and Indian
War had begun in 1754, and the Quakers, opposed to all wars, had
become victims of hostility from their neighbors who supported the
British war effort against the French. Callender's diary recorded that
when there was "a grand illumination" to celebrate a victory, "the
Quakers paid." The crowd "broke twenty panes of glass for us. Some
window shutters shattered to pieces."

Yet that spring day in the troubled year of 1759 gave Hannah Callender an interval of delight and freedom. She had come to New York and was taken to see Jamaica as a pleasant local town.

She went riding out this morning with a group of friends her own age. They "went to the beach" on Long Island. She noticed immediately the "fine white sand along it." The horses moved easily across the beach, on the strip of sand "so hard that riding makes no impression on it."

From time to time, the sea swept toward the racing horses, awesome in its power. These were not mere ripples by the shore; there was the power of the Atlantic in them as they hit the beach. Hannah Callender and her friends were riding right along the line where the sea met the land. This was a somewhat dangerous place, exciting, with a sense of risk. "The riding is so fine," she exclaimed.

The pure white sand and the beating waves, the distant hills and the nearby dunes, all came together to create "one of the most glorious sights my eyes ever beheld." Even the reminder of war, those alarm beacons on a hill, could not spoil that moment of happiness. The natural world was enough for a while to compensate for human folly.

That evening, further inland, the party climbed up to a high lookout at the top of a great tree. From there she had another view of the beach. She saw once more the place where she had been so happy. It reminded her that life had the promise of good moments in it.

The Source of the River

William Turner, diplomat, writing in his journal

ALONG THE MENDERES RIVER, TURKEY · NOVEMBER 17, 1816

We left [the town] at half past seven, and in two hours ascended to the source of the Mender Sou [Menderes]; for the first hour we rode along the plain at the foot of the mountain, which we ascended for the whole of the second; we rode mostly along the side of the river, and forded three streams which joined it from other sources; our road lay along high paths overhanging the river which was very rapid, troubled and tumultuous [. . .] as we rode to the source, we had light but frequent showers owing to the clouds breaking against the heights which were covered with them.

We reached the fall [and source] at half past nine; the scenery round it was of the wildest and most beautiful description; the water gushes out most copiously from a small square aperture in the rock, and falls about fifty feet over a bed of stone at an angle of about eighty-five; the width of the fall is about ten feet; above it the rock rises perpendicularly about 150 feet, with pines growing plentifully out of it; to the right of the fall rose another perpendicular crag of pine-clothed rock as high as that over it; the noise of the fall had a noble effect, and added much to the picturesque of the scene; to the right of the fall were several other streams gushing from smaller holes in the rock, and water poured copiously down from the mountains on every side, but these latter streams arise only from rain and melted snow, and are dry in summer.

⚬∞⚬

William Turner was in Turkey, setting out as a British diplomat. He was in his twenties, and this was his first post. Subsequently, in the 1820s, he was for a time the British ambassador in Constantinople. He later held a number of diplomatic postings elsewhere.

During his first years in Constantinople, Turner took several trips to explore the region. Here he was touring west-central Turkey and had come to the Menderes River. It was known more famously as the Maeander, whose windings had given their name to a verb in ancient Greek for a river's snaking course. The river was celebrated in Homer's *Iliad*. Turner, like all young men of his education in that period, knew the Greek classics.

As his party went up the mountain and closer to the source of the river, the water was making an ever-deeper impression on him. He thought about where it was all coming from. Rain and melted snow provided one origin. Scientific explanations aside, he felt simply the water's rush of power, its energy of moving.

The waterfall itself, marking the river's source, was not huge, yet "the noise of the fall had a noble effect" in its romantic setting, with the rock rising sheer above it and dotted with pine trees. The reason why this waterfall was special was not simply its immediate impact on the senses. Here the water was pouring out "from a small square aperture in the rock," with "several other streams gushing from smaller holes in the rock," and it all "poured copiously down from the mountains on every side." This was the source of a great river, whose power and permanence were emerging right here, from inside the earth, and then rushing down the mountain. There was something elemental about this sudden and continuous uproar.

It all gave William Turner a rich sensation of mind and senses. He was in the presence of the creativity of nature itself. He had ventured out in the pursuit of rational knowledge, but he had found something deeper: an experience of happiness in the presence of water as source of life.

Food and Drink

The Peerless Plum

Ibn Battuta, scholar and traveler,
speaking about China in his travel memoir

TANGIER, MOROCCO · CA. 1354

After a voyage of seventeen days, during which the wind was always favour-able, we arrived in China. This is a vast country, and it abounds in all sorts of good things [. . .] You find in China a great deal of sugar as good as that of Egypt, better in fact; you find also grapes and plums. I used to think that the plum called Othmani, which you get at Damascus, was peerless; but I found how wrong I was when I became acquainted with the plum of China. In this country there is also an excellent watermelon which is like that of Khwarezm and Ispahan. In short, all our fruits have their match in China, or rather they are excelled.

❧

Ibn Battuta was born in 1304 in Tangier. He came from a learned Moroccan family and was himself a scholar in law and other fields. But his lifelong passion was to travel, and he authored one of the great travel books of all time, the *Rihlah* (*Travels*), about the many places he had visited.

Ibn Battuta was destined for a relatively stationary life. But this changed during his pilgrimage to Mecca in 1325, when he decided to keep traveling afterwards. Three decades and tens of thousands of miles later, he came home to Morocco to tell his story. He dictated his many adventures to a clerk, summoning up in his mind all the moments of a lifetime spent exploring far from home.

After his initial pilgrimage to Mecca, instead of returning to Morocco, he had gone to Persia. The appetite whetted, he went to east-ern Africa, then to India, where he worked as a judge for the sultan in Delhi, which he thought a fine city. He spent years there and then was sent by the sultan on an embassy to China, which was for him an almost legendary country. The first attempt to get there failed; he was shipwrecked, and instead of China he saw what is now Sri Lanka. But eventually he succeeded in reaching his most distant destination.

Ibn Battuta was amazed by China. Most of his travels had taken him round the Islamic world, which at the time stretched from Spain to North Africa and Arabia, Persia through India. In China he admired the fields by the wide river, the corn, and the fruit trees.

He appreciated the tastes of this country. There was the Chinese sugar, "a great deal" of it. Tasting this sugar allowed him to compare China to Egypt, another fine source of sweet harvests. We can almost hear him considering the tastes, as the distinctive sugars crunched and dissolved in his mouth and again in his memory. On first encounter, the Chinese variety was "as good as that of Egypt," and then he decided it was "better in fact." There were other sweet treats, too, an abundance of fruit including grapes and watermelon.

Above all, there was a particular moment when he tasted a Chinese plum for the first time. He remembered the finest plum in Syria. When he had tasted that, he had been sure its sweetness was "peerless." Then he "became acquainted with the plum of China." The new taste burst upon him. It was sweetness unlike any other. The flavor of life itself.

Looking back many years later, it was such memories that confirmed for Ibn Battuta that his lifetime of travel had been worthwhile. Who else could compare the perhaps finest plums in the world—from Damascus and China?

His happiness was twofold. First, there was the taste sensation itself; then there was the joy of being able to compare tastes from across the world. The moment when he had tasted his first Chinese plum had been straightforward—and yet his whole life had been affirmed by it.

Home-Style Cooking on the Wagon Trail

Lodisa Frizzell, pioneer woman,
writing in her travel journal

ELM CREEK, NEBRASKA · MAY 27, 1852

We encamped in a beautiful place, on the bank of a stream called Elm Creek, under the shade of two large elm trees; here was good grass, plenty of the best of wood, and some water, for the creek was very low, and as the sun was 3 hours high or more, some went out hunting while the old doctor, Beth [Bethel], and I went to cooking; we soon had the best of a fire, cooked some meat and beans, stewed some apples and peaches, boiled some rice, and baked biscuit, and fried some crulls, and as I had a glass pickle jar full of sour milk, and plenty of salaratus [baking soda], I had as fine cakes as if I had been at home; and when they returned in the evening we had a general feast.

⌒◯⌒

On April 14, 1852, Lodisa Frizzell and her husband, Lloyd, had set out with their four sons from their home in Effingham County, Illinois. They were taking the wagon trails to California, where they were hoping to make a better life. Their journey would take them across Illinois and Missouri and then on the Oregon Trail to Pacific Springs in Wyoming, where they arrived in June. They had some cattle and a pony along with their wagon of belongings. (In December of 1852, confined by snow in their mountain cabin in northern California, Lodisa Frizzell would record the adventures of this spring journey.)

On May 27, they paused at Elm Creek, near Fort Kearney and the Platte River. At Fort Kearney, several trails from further east merged, forming one trail westward across Nebraska to Fort Laramie in Wyoming. In those years, the area around Fort Kearney was so busy with pioneers moving west that there was little grass left for the animals, and hardly any firewood. Disease was common.

But for Lodisa Frizzell, Elm Creek turned out to be a "beautiful place," with plenty of shade under "two large elm trees." Frizzell had with her an old doctor and her son Bethel. Her expert eye noticed the quality of the spot, "good grass, plenty of the best of wood, and some water." She began to get a delicious meal ready. Normally, lighting a camp fire was hard work on this trail. They had to dig a pit into the ground and then fill it with wood. Matches for lighting fires were precious. Here, on the banks of the creek, the fuel was handy and easy to light. She "soon had the best of a fire."

Since they were on the trail for months, they carried various cooking equipment with them. Lodisa Frizzell must have had a frying pan and also pots for boiling. She carefully cooked the various dishes over the open fire. One by one, she got it all ready.

First she cooked a staple of the Oregon Trail, meat and beans. Then she stewed the fruit. After that she did the boiling, then the baking, and finally the frying. The detail in her description is full of love. She was bringing her past domestic world back to life under the elm trees of the creek, surrounded by the vastness of Nebraska.

"Crulls," fried doughnuts, were a special treat. She listed the ingredients with glee: the jar of sour milk and the baking soda. When the doughnuts were ready, she had a moment of proud happiness, because she "had as fine cakes as if I had been at home." It was a triumph over difficult circumstances.

Eventually the rest of the party returned from hunting, and she had the satisfaction of treating them to "a general feast." For one evening, the dangers and uncertainties of the journey could be forgotten.

A Philosopher's Last Taste of Life

Hermippus, pupil of Epicurus,
writing a letter to friends

ISLAND OF LESBOS, GREECE · 270 BCE

He [Epicurus] died of the stone [. . .] after having been ill a fortnight; and at the end of the fortnight [. . .] he went into a brazen bath, properly tempered with warm water, and asked for a cup of pure wine and drank it; and having recommended his friends to remember his doctrines, he expired.

∽∞∾

The Greek philosopher Epicurus was born on the island of Samos in 341 BCE. When he was in his thirties, he set up a school of philosophy—in a garden—in Athens. He was a spiritual teacher and writer who believed that people should value ordinary pleasures. In 270 BCE, in Athens, he was dying of kidney stones. His friend and pupil Hermippus recorded the philosopher's last day (as quoted in the later writings of the Greek historian Diogenes Laertes).

Other sources show that Epicurus had made sure his will was right: the garden, his pride and joy, was left to a friend, on condition that it was used by those who wished to discuss philosophy. His house was likewise to be a home for a school. He took great care of the precise conditions.

His final day had come, and he probably spent it with friends. Having made sure of his will, he was able to give some thought to these—his very last—hours. Epicurus was famous (or notorious) among his contemporaries for his refusal to share religious belief. If there are gods, he taught, they have no interest in humanity. He had no consoling faith in an afterlife. For him, these were his last moments of consciousness.

First, there was the gleaming metal of the bath tub. Then the warm water was poured in. He ensured that the water was "properly tempered." A careful, simple moment.

As Epicurus sat in the bath tub, he felt for one last time the pleasant sensation of liquid warmth.

Then there came the last taste of life itself, for which everything else on this day of dying had been a preparation. During his sickness, Epicurus would have drunk his wine blended with water. Now he had no more need for precautions. Calmly, he requested a cup of "pure wine." Though later generations have accused him of excess, he was by all accounts a most moderate drinker. Raising the cup to his lips, he took his last mouthfuls of this drink that the Greeks thought of as a gift of the gods.

As he relished the taste, beyond the echoes of past pleasure, there must have been the present happiness of being a free man. He died as he had lived, choosing his own way. At the very end, he drew the attention of his friends and pupils to his philosophical ideas, which had guided him to his final moment.

Epicurus gave his own account of this last day in letters to friends such as Hermarchus. He seems to have been motivated by concern to make sure provision was made for the children of one of his friends, Metrodorus. He recorded calmly in one such letter that he had been very ill for seven days. Another conveyed the passing experience of the time with complete control: "Epicurus to Hermarchus, greeting. I write these words on the happiest, and the last, day of my life. I am suffering from diseases of the bladder and intestines, which are of the utmost possible severity. Yet all my sufferings are counterbalanced by the joy which I derive from remembering my theories and discoveries."

Life tasted good to the dying man as he relinquished the cup.

The Sea Air Gives a Good Appetite

Thomas Turner, village shopkeeper, writing in his diary

EAST HOATHLY, EAST SUSSEX · JUNE 24, 1764

In the morn, at thirty minutes past five, Thomas Durrant and I set out for Newhaven, to see my very worthy friend Mr. Tipper, where we arrived at fifty minutes past seven, and breakfasted with my friend Tipper; after which we walked down to the sea, where we entertained ourselves very agreeably an hour or two [. . .] We dined with my friend Tipper, on a leg of lamb boiled, a hot baked rice pudding, a gooseberry pie, a very fine lobster, green salad, and fine white cabbage. We stayed with my friend Tipper till thirty minutes past four, and then came away, and came home safe and well about three minutes past nine.

⸙

Thomas Turner was born in Kent in the year 1729; later, his family moved to Sussex. When he was in his early twenties, he became a village shopkeeper in East Hoathly, selling all the different things that people might need on a day-to-day basis. He was not wealthy and had to rent the shop premises. His first marriage had been stormy, though by 1764, when he had been a widower for three years, his memories were affectionate. It would not be long before he married a second time and also became the proud owner of his shop.

Turner was sociable and well-liked in the community, and he held various part-time posts, including that of undertaker, schoolmaster, and surveyor. He was also a voracious reader of classical and modern literature, and he kept an extraordinary diary. It reflects the vividness of a lively mind that was able to appreciate everyday experiences, including his personal frailties and limitations. Turner was always alive to the little things that made his life quietly rich.

He had risen early on that summer Sunday morning. Avoiding church for once (though he was a devout man), he and his friend Thomas Durrant "set out for Newhaven," a little town on the south coast. There another friend, Tipper, was awaiting them, and the three shared breakfast together. It was a cheerful beginning of a good day.

They walked together "down to the sea" where they breathed in the sea air and larked about. Turner had worked very long days for much of his life. It was hard to build up any kind of savings. These moments of freedom were rare—they must have felt like a precious holiday.

The salty air, the hours of walking, gave Thomas Turner a good appetite that Sunday. When the friends came back to Tipper's home, a real feast was awaiting them. It was Sunday lunch, but with lots of special dishes added. There was the hot sweetness of the pudding, the tartness of the gooseberry pie. The lobster was surely fresh here by the sea. There was a crisp salad, and even the cabbage was fine.

It was not really any one dish that made the occasion so splendid for Thomas Turner on that special Sunday. There was the warm atmosphere, "with my friend Tipper." He also felt a lively play of contrasts, tastes, and textures—sea and land, green and white, hot and cold. He was a man who was able to enjoy what was in front of him, on its own terms. He loved any number of particulars, the sequence of sensations that came to him on a good day. And he understood that many details, woven together, created lasting experiences: this Sunday lunch was so fine because they had enjoyed walking by the sea, which in turn had been fine because they had had such a nice breakfast with their friend.

The enjoyment of the meals and the walk stretched into the afternoon spent together. He and Durrant must have been very reluctant to set off for home, and so it was past nine by the time they were back in their village. It was quite late, given how early he had to begin work the next day. But the outing had been worthwhile indeed. He had recovered the taste of life itself. He was ready for another week of hard work.

A Handful of Refreshing Well Water

Lady Sarashina, court attendant, composing a memoir of a childhood journey

KYOTO, JAPAN · CA. 1050s

Around the end of the fourth month, I had to move to a place in the Eastern Hills. Some of the rice paddies that I passed on the way had been irrigated, while in others the seedlings had been planted; the green of the fields made for a charming sight [. . .]

As the place was near Ryozen Temple, a friend and I went there to pray. The walk there was most strenuous, and so we stopped by the stone well near the temple. As we scooped the water up with our hands, my friend said, "I don't think I could ever get enough of this fresh water." I asked in reply, "Deep in the mountains, you raise up water from between the rocks—is it only now that you realise you cannot get enough of it?" [. . .]

On the way back the evening sun shone bright, and we could see all of the capital.

⁓⧖⁓

Lady Sarashina (also known as Sugawara no Takasue no Musume, meaning the daughter of Sugawara Takasue) was an attendant at the Japanese court in Kyoto. Her father had been an assistant governor in the province of Kazusa.

In this diary-style memoir, Lady Sarashina recorded a three-month journey from the provinces back to the capital that had taken place in around 1020, when she was a girl. This is an older woman's vivid memory of an important event in her childhood.

They had set out for Kyoto on a foggy evening. The young girl had cried when she got into the carriage. She was anxious, too, about how she might be regarded in the capital city, having lived in a remote province far to the east. Would the people at court not think she was uncultured?

The journey was long, with many hardships compared to her normal life. Sometimes the rain fell so fiercely that their lodgings were wet, and she was so frightened of floods that she could not sleep.

On this day, near the end of their journey, things had begun to feel better. Their next temporary home was located "in the Eastern Hills." Looking out at the fields as they went past, she enjoyed the fresh green that came from irrigation.

She went to a nearby Buddhist temple, taking a friend. Tired after this walk, as well as from the whole journey, she went to have a drink of water from a stone well. This was quite certainly not how she normally took a drink. Having no cup, the friends "scooped the water up" with their hands.

There were two great pleasures in that gesture: it was a shared experience, and it was so perfectly simple. After much anxiety and gloom on the road, a handful of fresh water satisfied the most basic of human needs.

They both enjoyed the pure taste of the well water, and the friend admitted, "'I don't think I could ever get enough of this fresh water.'" The young Lady Sarashina replied by using an apt quotation from a poem about being in the mountains and raising up water from between rocks. It was a deeply natural satisfaction, originating with the fundamental elements of water and stone.

Throughout the journey, there had been dangers and fears. Now there was a sense of harmony and of being at home. Fresh water—nothing more, nothing less—gave her this gift of belonging.

It was evening when they returned from the temple and saw the capital city, illuminated by the glow of the setting sun. It, too, was no longer frightening. A moment of happiness at a stone well had changed her outlook.

A Tasty Dinner in a Rustic Tavern

Cyrus P. Bradley, college student,
writing in his travel diary

NEAR SANDUSKY, OHIO · JUNE 14, 1835

Last evening, the agent assured us we should be in Sandusky. But it rained all the afternoon; there was a violent thunderstorm and the aspect of affairs became really discouraging. About nine o'clock, we stopped at a log hut to exchange our horses, when our new driver (for we change drivers here with the teams) [. . .] came out and declared with many emphatic asseverations that it would be absolutely impossible to get across the prairie that night [. . .] As we saw he was determined not to proceed, we gave up the case [. . .]

The log hut [. . .] was called a tavern; a bar well stocked with whiskey. At one end was a generous fire in a fireplace of true primitive capacity and here we sat and laughed at the awkwardness of our situation and poured maledictions upon those whose lies had been instrumental in bringing us here. Better had we not left the canal. Our boat doubtless [had already] arrived at Cleveland [. . .]

However, we forgot our cares over a good supper of roast venison, corn bread and fresh butter, and then enquired for lodging. There were many awkward grimaces made, as we all, one by one, poked up the crazy ladder into a dark hole of undefined dimensions, called par eminence the chamber. Here in the garret of a log hut, about a dozen persons passed the night—the day had been rainy and the floor and the beds flowed with water. I managed to obtain a dry couch, and as I lay on my back, could contemplate the beauties of the starry creation or calculate an almanac through the chinks of the massive, rough-fitted logs which formed the roof and walls of the house.

However, I slept soundly, and at five o'clock, we [. . .] emerged.

⸎

Cyrus P. Bradley was born in September 1818, in Canterbury, New Hampshire. He was raised, he wrote in his journal, "in the woods" where, lacking boys to play with, he "found company in everything, in the birds, in the old cat, the cow," and other animals. By June of 1835, he had grown into a lively and extremely articulate young man.

He had enrolled at Dartmouth College, but his health was poor. A trustee of Dartmouth suggested and arranged this trip for Cyrus, hoping that it would help to restore his health.

Cyrus made his way to Pittsburgh and then down the Ohio River to Cincinnati. In early June, he took a boat on the Ohio River to Portsmouth and then on, via the Scioto River, to Columbus. But this trip was from the start beset with delays. Growing impatient with the slow progress, he and some fellow travelers decided to leave the canal boat and take a coach overland. But further difficulties and delays beset them and so they found themselves arriving in the late evening of June 13 at this tavern, and still short of the town of Sandusky, which had been their goal.

The plan had been just to change horses and then complete this leg of the increasingly wearing journey. But the new driver, whom Cyrus described with some nervousness as "a great, strapping, bare-legged" fellow, refused absolutely to take them anywhere in the dark. Cyrus was stranded in this rudimentary log hut for the night.

There was a generous stock of whiskey and the warmth of a basic but roaring fire. He and his companions sat and "laughed at the awkwardness" of their frustrating situation and cursed the agent who had sent them on this detour. But then Cyrus's mood changed completely and his good spirits were more than restored in a short time. It was the joy of a good dinner that had this instantly restorative effect.

The ingredients of the dinner were homemade and tasty, and that was an essential element of the charm and pleasure of the experience: "roast venison, corn bread and fresh butter." These must have been local products. This "good supper" was a tonic, particularly for a young man whose health was poor. It was the simple richness of life itself that he enjoyed in that tavern on an unpredicted overnight stay.

After that fine meal, the continued inconveniences of the place seemed merely amusing, no longer upsetting. They climbed up to the garret where their bedding was waiting. Instead of worrying about the rainwater everywhere, Cyrus Bradley was fortunate enough to take possession of a dry couch and then looked up and "could contemplate the beauties of the starry creation" through the holes in the roof. Then he fell asleep.

The dinner of roast venison, corn bread, and fresh butter had transformed a bad evening into a special night.

The Excellence of Marinaded Pilchards

Humphry Davy, chemist and physicist, writing a letter home

BRISTOL · NOVEMBER 19, 1800

My dear mother—

Had I believed that my silence of six weeks would have given you a moment's uneasiness, I should have written long ago. But I have been engaged in my favourite pursuit of experimenting, and in endeavouring to amuse two of my friends who have spent some days at the Institute [. . .]

Accept my affectionate thanks for your presents. I have received them all, and I have made a good use of them all. Several times has a supper on the excellent marinaded pilchards made me recollect former times, when I sat opposite to you, my dear mother, in the little parlour, round the little table eating of the same delicious food, and talking of future unknown things. Little did I then think of my present situation, or of the mode in which I am, and am to be, connected with the world. Little did I then think I should ever be so long absent from the place of my birth as to feel longings so powerful as I now feel for visiting it again.

I shall see with heartfelt pleasure the time approaching when I shall again behold my first home—when I shall endeavour to repay some of the debts of gratitude I owe to you, to the Doctor [Tonkin], and to my aunts. My next visit shall not be so short a one as the last. I will stay with you at least two or three months. You have let half your house. Have you a bedroom reserved for me, and a little room for a laboratory?

⌁∞⌁

When he wrote this letter home to his mother in Penzance, Cornwall, twenty-one-year-old Humphry Davy was working in a newly founded scientific institution in the English city of Bristol, where he was devising experiments on the recently discovered "laughing gas" and on an early version of the electrical battery. His research on voltage would become the first of his papers to be published in the Royal Society's *Philosophical Transactions*. He was appointed to the Royal Institution in London in 1801, where his work on electricity made him world-famous. Davy was not from a wealthy background and he was largely self-educated, with the support of his mother and Dr. John Tonkin, a local surgeon. All along, Davy remained proud of his Cornish roots.

Soon he would be in London. But already in Bristol, the young scientist was far away from his family in Cornwall and intensely immersed in his research. Thus, not surprisingly, he had forgotten to write home. Now he was eager to remedy the fault.

His anxious mother had sent a parcel of treats—and he had not replied in six weeks. He was indeed feeling guilty.

But, as he explained in this letter, though he had been too distracted to write before, it had not stopped him from enjoying the food she had sent. He had dined well "on the excellent marinaded pilchards," a treat he must have anticipated after the hard work in the laboratory in Bristol. The pilchards, little sardines, had been marinaded to preserve them. This also preserved the taste of home for him. As another writer from the period put it, "pilchards are to Cornwall what herrings are to Yarmouth, cotton to Manchester and coals to Newcastle." This writer added that one could smell "the odour of pilchards" everywhere in a Cornish town, "in every corner, cottage, lane, loft, room, inn, chapel, and church thereof."

For Davy, the pilchards were a flavor reminiscent of his earlier years. They had made him "recollect former times, when I sat opposite to you, my dear mother, in the little parlour." On those evenings in the past, "eating of the same delicious food," he had talked excitedly of "future unknown things." Now those dreams were on the verge of becoming real by his impending appointment in London. The taste of the fish had brought back the old days and reaffirmed the values with which he had been brought up. He was happy in the present moment, which was filled with the happiness of the past.

A Great Plenty of Party Treats

Anna Winslow, schoolgirl,
writing a letter home to her mother

BOSTON · JANUARY 17, 1772

There was a large company assembled in a handsome, large, upper room in the new end of the house [. . .] Our treat was nuts, raisins, cakes, wine, punch, hot and cold, all in great plenty. We had a very agreeable evening from five to ten o'clock. For variety we woo'd a widow, hunted the whistle, threaded the needle [various parlour games], and while the company was collecting, we diverted ourselves with playing of pawns; no rudeness, Mamma, I assure you. Aunt Deming desires you would particularly observe that the elderly part of the company were spectators only, they mixed not in either of the above described scenes.

I was dressed in my yellow coat, black bib and apron, black feathers on my head, my paste [imitation gems] comb, and all my paste garnet marquesite and jet pins, together with my silver plume—my locket, rings, black collar round my neck, black mitts and 2 or 3 yards of blue ribbon (black and blue is high taste), striped tucker and ruffles (not my best) and my silk shoes completed my dress.

⌒∞⌒

Anna Winslow was about eleven years old, writing long letters from Boston home to her mother in Halifax, Nova Scotia. Anna had grown up in Halifax, where her father served in the British army. Both parents were originally from Boston, and they had sent their daughter to stay there with an aunt for the proper "schooling." Anna had arrived in 1770 and was by now part of the Boston scene; she particularly enjoyed the parties.

Her best friend was Hannah Soley. Together, they had planned a party at the Soley household, "a very genteel, well-regulated assembly." They thought out dances, food, drink, games, and the guest list—all girls, from good Boston families. Following the dancing, there was a busy schedule of pleasures. It was great fun and so, for the future, Anna was careful to add, "no rudeness, Mamma."

Part of her happiness that evening was the culinary "treat." She loved all the little things that composed it, the hospitable spread of "nuts, raisins, cakes." Nuts and raisins were very much eighteenth-century party food, sweet things for a special occasion, and they were probably used in the cakes as well. There were special drinks, too, "wine, punch, hot and cold."

Taken together, the nuts and raisins, the cakes and punch, made up her idea of "great plenty." It felt to Anna as if the world had no greater riches to offer. It was simply perfect.

Another part of her happiness was her party dress. It was not unlike the "treat," being made up of colorful details, all equally appealing and satisfying. She had her "yellow coat, black bib and apron, black feathers on my head." She adored the comb and plume, the locket and ribbon, which had the "high taste" color of blue. Her "silk shoes" were the finishing touch, completing her "dress." They completed her happiness, too.

Her aunt joined in the letter, careful to assure Anna's mother that the grown-ups had remained dignified and quiet. In other letters, Anna admitted to being so full of laughter that her aunt, who was sitting by her as she wrote, said she could get no sense out of her at all.

Anna Winslow loved writing about vivid details of her life in Boston such as the party "treat" and her clothes. The prospect of writing her experiences down, and the promise of their being read at home, made her life more interesting to her—and her moments of happiness all the deeper.

Well-Being

A Landscape Fit for a Stroll

Thomas Green, country gentleman, writing in his diary

LONDON · JUNE 10, 1798

Escaped out of the crowd and bustle, and strolled to Richmond. Passed on our way, by Ham Common, an extraordinary elm, called Ham Church: two thirds of its enormous trunk decayed away; the remainder pierced through; but the top still exuberant. Ascended Richmond Terrace, and enjoyed perhaps the most richly variegated scene in English landscape. Returned by the Thames, and paused, with much interest, opposite [Alexander] Pope's villa and garden: his favourite willow on the lawn, propped up by stakes.

✦

Thomas Green lived in the market town of Ipswich, near the east coast of England, where he had received his early education. Poor health had prevented him from becoming a student at Cambridge University, but instead he had qualified as a lawyer in London. For a time he had practiced as a barrister in Norfolk. Then his father died in 1794, and thereafter Green led a private and scholarly life in the family home in Ipswich, keeping a diary devoted to his literary interests and his love of landscape. Now, in his late twenties, he was taking a trip to London and the surrounding areas.

The city was even busier than usual. There were many preparations going on for the war with Napoleon, adding to the normal business and hustle. Green was glad to leave the uproar and activity behind: "Escaped out of the crowd and bustle, and strolled." This word, "strolled," transformed both his mindset and his surroundings. Everything was slowed down and stretched out. Leisureliness in nature replaced the unwelcome urban intensity of the day so far. Strolling was the expression of his general approach to life, one that made him receptive to passing moments in all their curiosity. At home, he spent much of his time "strolling" through books and noting down passages of value. Here he wrote down the impressions left by that easy, unhurried wandering, free of the tensions of city life.

His outing took him along the River Thames toward what was at that period the little town of Richmond, southwest of central London. First he was impressed and moved by an old elm called Ham Church, "the top still exuberant" despite the old age of the decaying trunk. His route then took him up Richmond Terrace, part of a hill famous for its view of the Thames and its surroundings. There he was able to appreciate a perspective that he savored with trained enthusiasm as "perhaps the most richly variegated scene in English landscape."

In the early eighteenth century, the renowned Dutch landscape painter Leonard Knyff had depicted the view from Richmond Hill as a fine example of picturesque scenery. This tradition then influenced the unfolding English landscape genre as established by Thomas Gainsborough, George Stubbs, and others. Thomas Green enjoyed this view as if it were a painting partly due to that artistic development, and partly because of the variety and the subtlety of its details: the blend of riverside and hill, meadows and fine dwellings—such as the house of the famous early-eighteenth-century poet Alexander Pope. Many eighteenth-century writers, too, praised the English countryside for its picturesque scenes and its varying features that made such strolls as satisfying as this one was for Thomas Green.

A bit later, he walked along the river to appreciate more closely the residence and garden where Pope had lived at Twickenham, just across the river from Richmond. Here he saw a weeping willow, planted by the poet in his famous "grotto," a secluded garden referred to in his poetry as an escape from the bustle and distractions of society. Weeping willows, from Turkey, had been introduced into England in about 1700, around the time this one had been planted.

Another writer at the time remarked that Pope's willow was "propped with uncommon care." Thomas Green, too, was impressed and later reflected with amusement that "great men should plant trees of greater duration."

These were strolling thoughts indeed, each one a source of reflection and pleasure. The whole walk had turned into one extended moment of happiness during which he "paused, with much interest," to enjoy not only specific sights but through them the larger world.

The Joy of Coming Home

Seydi Ali Reis, commander,
writing in his travel memoir

ISTANBUL, TURKEY · 1556

From there our way led past Ghekivize and Skutari [on the eastern shore of the Bosphorus], where I crossed the Bosphorus, and reached Constantinople [Istanbul] in safety.

God be praised, who led me safely through manifold dangers, and brought me back to this most beautiful country of all the earth. Four years have passed away; years of much sorrow and misery, of many privations and perplexities; but now in this year 964 [1556 CE], in the beginning of [the month of] Redjeb, I have once more returned to my own people, my relations, and my friends. Glory and praise be to God the Giver of all good things!

⁂

In 1552, when he was in his fifties, Seydi Ali Reis had been made commander of the Ottoman fleet in the Indian Ocean, during a war with the Portuguese. It was immediately following a terrible defeat at sea that had led to the replacement of the previous Ottoman commander. Seydi Ali Reis was an experienced soldier and sailor, as well as the author of books on astronomy and navigation. But he, too, suffered substantial losses in another naval battle against the Portuguese. Separated from the rest of the fleet, and eventually reaching Gujarat in western India, it took him four years to return to Constantinople. He reached it, at last, on this glad day in 1556.

He had had many adventures in India and the eastern seas. He had witnessed the worst and the best of humanity. He had seen terrible armed fights and many deaths, particularly in that first sea battle: "Five of our galleys and as many of the enemy's boats were sunk and utterly wrecked, one of theirs went to the bottom with all sails set. In a word, there was great loss on both sides." He had also seen the destructive powers of nature and their terrifying impact: "It was truly a terrible day, but at last we reached Gujarat in India, which part of it, however, we knew not, when the pilot suddenly exclaimed: 'On your guard! a whirlpool in front!' Quickly the anchors were lowered, but the ship was dragged down." The long journey back home had been as terrifying as the original battles and the subsequent odyssey.

Sometimes he had been welcomed with graceful hospitality. But often, he had been hunted like an animal, escaping by chance and daring. The only thing more dangerous than the climate and the terrain had been some of the local people.

When Seydi Ali Reis finally reentered the Ottoman realm, he encountered more familiar places. At last, he reached the strait of the Bosphorus and saw his native city rising up on the opposite shore.

As he crossed the strait, he must have realized all he had passed through—"safely through manifold dangers." Perhaps he relived, as if in one rush, all the fear and the loss, the isolation and the suffering. He had been caught by a typhoon at sea; he had scaled mountains on rough tracks; he had had his way blocked by bands of robbers; he had been tricked and had to defend himself in strange courts. Now that was all behind him.

Relief filled his soul. He saw his home and felt complete. He had come blessedly "back to this most beautiful country of all the earth." For him, this was no empty expression. Compared to most men at the time, he had seen many countries of the world. He could truly compare his experience of coming home with the impressions of many other places.

He felt a strong sense of belonging: "I have once more returned to my own people." They were waiting to welcome him back, "my relations, and my friends" as well as the government officials. It was a moment of supreme restoration. He gave praise to God as the source of "all good things." It was in that moment of return as if he had received every good thing he knew in the world—all at once. It was the happiness of coming home.

A World in Bloom

Pehr Kalm, naturalist, writing in his botanical journal

SWEDESBORO, NEW JERSEY · APRIL 20, 1749

This day I found the strawberries in flower, for the first time this year; the fruit is commonly larger than that in Sweden but it seems to be less sweet and agreeable.

The annual [cereal] harvest, I am told, is always of such a nature that it affords plenty of bread for the inhabitants, though it turns out to greater advantage in some years than it does in others. A venerable septuagenary Swede called Aoke Helm assured me that in his time no absolutely barren crop had been met with, but that the people had always had pretty plentiful crops [. . .]

The peach trees were now everywhere in blossom; their leaves were not yet come out of the buds, and therefore the flowers showed to greater advantage; their beautiful pale red colour had a very fine effect and they sat so close that the branches were entirely clad with them. The other fruit trees were not yet in flower; however, the apple blossoms began to appear.

⁙

Pehr Kalm was the son of a Swedish pastor. He was born in 1716 and lived for most of his life in the Swedish-speaking community in Finland. Though from a poor background, he received strong support from teachers and professors—one of whom was the famous botanist Carolus Linnaeus—during a promising academic career. By the time he was thirty, he was a professor of economics at the academy in Turku, Finland. He was also a member of the Royal Swedish Academy of Sciences.

It was the Swedish Academy that sent him in September 1748 on a trip to North America. It had several different purposes. Since he was an expert botanist, he was asked to survey the plant life of the continent. He was also to report on social developments, particularly among the large number of migrants from Sweden. He had letters of introduction to eminent Americans, and he did in fact befriend Benjamin Franklin.

Kalm kept a journal during his stay in North America that lasted from September 1748 until February 1751. He included many botanical details, since this was at the core of his work. But at the same time, in a plain and modest fashion, he also gave expression to his feelings about the visit and the new world it was disclosing to him.

When he wrote this passage, he was living in the Swedish community of Raccoon (now Swedesboro) in southern New Jersey. This was where he observed his first American spring. After what had certainly been a long and hard winter, the signs of the warmer season were now all around him. The first fruit blossom was out, and the strawberries were "in flower."

He must have asked the Swedish settlers if the strawberries fulfilled their promise, and they were rather critical of this American variant, preferring the old Scandinavian berries that they remembered. This led to some pleasant conversation about the area and its agriculture. Here the advantages of the New World began to emerge. The elderly Mr. Helm was clearly somebody Kalm trusted to be truthful when he declared that this was a place that gave them "pretty plentiful crops." The implied contrast was with their native land, where cereal harvests had sometimes failed and led to hardship and even famine in the eighteenth century. New Jersey might have strawberries that were less sweet, but on the other hand they were bigger, and the cereal harvests were also on a generous scale.

It was as if Kalm absorbed this sense of plenty around him and began to see this strange place differently. He looked up and saw the spring suddenly all around him. The peach trees were "everywhere in blossom"; "their beautiful pale red colour had a very fine effect."

He looked more closely. The blossoms seemed to hug the branches tightly, there were so many of them. These trees were fitting symbols of the place, gently fertile and neat and with the promise of a good harvest. This was a world fit for living—and he was happy to be part of it.

Pehr Kalm got married as well while he was in Raccoon. He brought back to Sweden and Finland more than a fine scholarly record of North America. Life itself blossomed for this sensitive scientist in the New Jersey countryside in the spring of 1749.

Home, Sweet Home

Jane Welsh Carlyle, diarist and writer,
composing a letter to a friend

LONDON · AUGUST 1836

*I ought not to regret my flight into Scotland since it has made me take with
new relish to London. It is a strange praise to bestow on the Metropolis of the
world, but I find it so delightfully still here! Not so much as a cock crowing to
startle nervous subjects out of their sleep; and during the day no inevitable
Mrs. this or Miss that, brimful of all the gossip for twenty miles around, inter-
rupting your serious pursuits (whatever they may be) with calls of a duration
happily unknown in cities. The feeling of calm, of safety, of liberty which came
over me on re-entering my own house was really the most blessed I had felt for
a great while.*

Jane Baillie Welsh was born in 1801 and moved from her native Scotland to London in 1834, some eight years after marrying the historian Thomas Carlyle. She was now in her middle thirties, a lively and
independent spirit in the social and intellectual world of literary London. Their marriage had its strains, though, since both of them were
subject to moods of doubt and depression. They were not always at
ease with one another, yet they also had a deep dialogue through all
the ups and downs.

Jane Carlyle had been suffering from ill health and in 1836 had
decided to take a trip home to rural Scotland, hoping that she would
recover there, free from the strains of urban life. Now, after a few
months, she had come back home to their house in Chelsea, in the
heart of London. In this letter to her friend Miss Hunter, she recorded
her astonished happiness at returning to her Chelsea home in the
"Metropolis of the world."

She began by admitting that she now felt a "new relish" for the city
from which she had been trying to escape. Her taste for this urban
world, the excitement she had felt when she had first arrived here, had
returned. She was amused at herself and her laughter can be heard

behind her words. She realized that her friend, and indeed most people, would assume that the rural life was quiet and peaceful, the urban life full of noise and stress. But to her, on the contrary, it was a delight not to be woken by the crowing of the cock, which stood in her witty way for the whole "hubbub" of country living. Then she picked out the apparently friendly neighbors, who would have been regarded as a virtue of rural life by many other people. The countryside did not mean friendliness to her either, any more than peace. She was just relieved to have no more visitors to deal with, and no more seemingly endless gossiping conversations to endure!

With a touch of self-mocking humor, Jane Carlyle realized she was not presenting herself in a very appealing light—but she could not help it. She was just so glad to be back in London.

When she came to record the moment of her arrival at home, she dropped the wit and the playfulness from her letter. She was simply overwhelmed by the joyful sensation of being back in her Chelsea house. She had a sudden and all-encompassing "feeling of calm, of safety, of liberty," and it transformed her whole perspective on her life.

This was a moment of happiness that had a beautifully balanced quality. She was at ease; she felt relieved of the anxiety that belonged to her experience of the world beyond London. But more than that, she felt confident now, light and able to move around. She was back in her own space. She was realizing, as if for the first time, just how happy this home could be.

A Traveler's Sweeping Prospect

Benjamin of Tudela, rabbi and traveler, composing his travel account

TUDELA, SPAIN · CA. 1173

From the Valley of Jehoshaphat the traveller immediately ascends the Mount of Olives, as this valley only intervenes between the city [Jerusalem] and the mount. From hence the Dead Sea is distinctly visible. Two parasangs [ancient measurement of distances] from the sea stands the salt pillar into which Lot's wife was metamorphosed; and although the sheep continually lick it, the pillar grows again, and retains its original state. You also have a prospect over the whole valley of the Dead Sea, and of the brook of Shittim, even as far as Mount Nebo.

⸻

Benjamin of Tudela was born in 1130 in the Jewish community of Tudela, Spain, the son of a distinguished rabbi. Though he also became a rabbi, he left his town and country around 1165 and embarked on a journey through parts of Europe, Asia, and North Africa. He returned to Spain in around 1173. His record of that journey became a celebrated travel book.

In twelfth-century Europe, most people spent their whole lives in one place. Aristocrats, clergy, and pilgrims were the exception. Journeys were physically difficult, the roads poor and the countryside dangerous. There was also a deeper reason why journeys such as Benjamin's were few. Knowledge came from tradition and from the authority of old and revered books; personal experience was not regarded as a useful basis for understanding the world.

Benjamin of Tudela was a learned man who had studied all the authorities in Jewish tradition. His father, Jonah, was a leading figure in Spanish Judaism. Yet the son decided to find out about the world— and about Jewish communities in different places—for himself. He did not do this to challenge the established order. Everywhere he went, across Europe, the Middle East, and beyond, he consulted the appropriate sources and listened to local authorities. Yet he did look for himself, too, and this led to some very personal and fulfilling moments.

This passage describes his arrival near Jerusalem in around 1170—the city that was holy, as he knew, to Jews, Christians, and Muslims.

The hills and valleys over and through which he walked carried names stretching back many centuries in the Hebrew texts. He climbed the Mount of Olives, noting that only one valley separated it from the city of Jerusalem.

From the summit, he saw that "the Dead Sea is distinctly visible." This moment was personal and moving and had an unmistakable tang of happiness. Looking round from the top of the Mount of Olives, he really could see the water in the distance, even "a prospect over the whole valley of the Dead Sea." Not far from it, he thought he identified the biblical pillar of salt that Lot's wife had become (this was perhaps a combination of local lore and scripture). Here he was, a man taking in an amazing view, a world stretching all around him.

He had walked this day on sacred and historic ground. He had gone to the Mount of Olives, where generations of Jews had their tombs, including, it was said, some of the prophets. It was to this mount that King David had fled during a crisis in his life.

From the top, Benjamin of Tudela could also discern Mount Nebo, where it was written that Moses was granted a glimpse of the Promised Land. It may even have been, so scholars said, his divinely ordained burial place.

His perspective swept across time as well as space. Hard to believe there was so much of the world! Difficult to believe that he was really there, in that place, seeing it all for himself! It is no wonder that such moments gave him a unique authority of his own, such as could almost rival the ancient texts, as the original preface to his travel account acknowledged: "The above-mentioned Rabbi Benjamin was a man of wisdom and understanding, and of much information; and after strict inquiry his words were found to be true and correct, for he was a true man."

In these words, the deep satisfaction of the intrepid traveler shone through the scholarly text. What greater happiness could there be for a man driven to cross oceans and deserts, ridges and valleys, when almost everybody else stayed close to home?

The Joy of Finding a Vocation

Jarena Lee, traveling preacher,
writing a personal memoir

PHILADELPHIA · 1836

The Rev. Richard Williams was to preach at Bethel Church, where I with others were assembled. He entered the pulpit, gave out the hymn, which was sung, and then addressed the throne of grace; took his text, passed through the exordium, and commenced to expound it. The text he took is in Jonah, 2nd chap. 9th verse—"Salvation is of the Lord." But as he proceeded to explain, he seemed to have lost the spirit; when in the same instant, I sprang, as by altogether supernatural impulse, to my feet, when I was aided from above to give an exhortation on the very text which my brother Williams had taken.

I told them I was like Jonah; for it had been then nearly eight years since the Lord had called me to preach his gospel to the fallen sons and daughters of Adam's race, but that I had lingered like him, and delayed to go at the bidding of the Lord, and warn those who are as deeply guilty as were the people of Nineveh.

During the exhortation, God made manifest his power in a manner sufficient to show the world that I was called to labor according to my ability, and the grace given unto me, in the vineyard of the good husbandman.

I now sat down, scarcely knowing what I had done, being frightened. I imagined that for this indecorum, as I feared it might be called, I should be expelled from the church. But instead of this, the Bishop [Richard Allen] rose up in the assembly, and related that I had called upon him eight years before, asking to be permitted to preach, and that he had put me off; but that he now as much believed that I was called to that work, as any of the preachers present. These remarks greatly strengthened me, so that my fears of having given an offence, and made myself liable as an offender, subsided, giving place to a sweet serenity, a holy joy of a peculiar kind, untasted in my bosom until then.

⁂

Jarena Lee was born to free African American parents in New Jersey in 1783. She was sent early to work as a servant and had little formal schooling. By 1818, she was a widow with two children of her own, living in Philadelphia.

Years before, she had asked the pastor of Bethel Church in Philadelphia, the Rev. Richard Allen (who would become the first bishop of the African Methodist Episcopal Church), for permission to fulfill her sense of vocation by preaching. He had refused. But on this Sunday in about 1818, she felt called again.

The minister that day, the Rev. Richard Williams, was getting ready to preach. Then he paused or stumbled. Jarena Lee stood up and took the theme of his text, "Salvation is of the Lord." This was her moment. Words sprang into her mind. There were no women preachers in this church. But today she felt called by God to address her congregation, publicly.

Thinking of Jonah, who held back from preaching the message of the Lord, she "told them I was like Jonah." Now she had found her own voice, and was able to keep going because "the Lord had called me to preach his gospel." Her words were flowing, mixing her own story with the text of the Bible. Her voice must have been ringing around the whole church, a great burst of expression that she had held in for so long.

When she was done, though, she expected a hostile response. She sat down again, "frightened." Instead, Bishop Allen himself, the man who had refused her previous request, rose to declare her spiritual right to speak. "He now as much believed that I was called to that work." That was a moment of affirmation that her inner power was unquestionable. Before the entire congregation, their bishop endorsed with all his authority her lonely assertion of the spiritual force within her.

From Jarena Lee's heart flowed an absolute happiness, the peace of being herself in the world. In that blessed finale to her daring, she felt her fears "giving place to a sweet serenity, a holy joy of a peculiar kind, untasted in my bosom until then." She became one of the first black women to preach, traveling to many places to address various audiences, and also holding prayer meetings. Through that one moment of joyous assurance, she now had gained the courage for a lifetime.

Winter Sunshine on a Warm Wall

George Eliot, novelist, writing a letter to a friend

GRANADA, SPAIN • FEBRUARY 21, 1867

We have had perfect weather ever since the 27th of January—magnificent skies and a summer sun. At Alicante, walking among the palm trees, with the bare brown rocks and brown houses in the background, we fancied ourselves in the Tropics; and a gentleman who travelled with us, assured us that the aspect of the country closely resembled Aden on the Red Sea. Here, at Granada, of course it is much colder, but the sun shines uninterruptedly; and in the middle of the day, to stand in the sunshine against a wall, reminds me of my sensations at Florence in the beginning of June. The aspect of Granada as we first approached it was a slight disappointment to me, but the beauty of its position can hardly be surpassed. To stand on one of the towers of the Alhambra and see the sun set behind the dark mountains of Loja, and send its afterglow on the white summits of the Sierra Nevada, while the lovely Vega [fertile plain] spreads below, ready to yield all things pleasant to the eye and good for food, is worth a very long, long journey. We shall start tomorrow evening for Cordova—then we shall go to Seville, back to Cordova, and on to Madrid.

George Eliot, the pen name of Mary Ann Evans, was forty-seven when she went on this winter vacation to Spain. She wrote back to her friend and publisher, John Blackwood, in rainy London. A few years ago, his firm had published Eliot's novels *Adam Bede*, *The Mill on the Floss*, and *Silas Marner*, and in the process he and Eliot had gotten to know and like each other. One of the reasons she had come to Spain was to try and complete a long poem that she would publish the following year as *The Spanish Gypsy*.

The trip to Spain also had more personal motives. She was traveling with her partner, George Henry Lewes. They had been a couple since 1853, though he had been unable to obtain a divorce from his wife and so could not marry Eliot. This made their relationship scandalous in the rigid world of polite England. But it did not stop her from being a popular author, who had earned enough to make such trips possible.

Lewes's health had weakened, and so she brought him to find some warmth and respite from London's winter, the fog and damp.

Here in Spain, the sun was shining brightly and the whole sky lit up and was "magnificent." Eliot had a feeling of space. This country was wonderful and simple and full of new experiences.

In Alicante, on the Mediterranean shore, the palm trees and the brown rocks made her feel as if they had left Europe and gone far south. In Granada, one of the beautiful cities of Andalusia, the whole of her pleasure in being here was present in one simple moment: "in the middle of the day, to stand in the sunshine against a wall." At that poised hour, when the day was almost summery, she could stand against a wall and just let the sunshine fall on her. This was as simple as any human experience could be. It was a moment of pure sensation: the warmth and the texture of the wall at her back and the sun on her face.

This almost tactile feeling reminded Eliot of her "sensations at Florence in the beginning of June." Perhaps she closed her eyes. This way she could more readily bring back the memory of Italy and blend it with the experience here and now in Spain. The comparison of sunshine and warmth was a way for her body to think and feel and remember.

George Eliot was one of the most intellectually engaged nineteenth-century novelists and also a journalist of ideas. She was a philosopher of politics and psychology. Here she had the unusual happiness of shaking off all complexity and just taking in the sensation of warming sunshine on a winter's day.

A Peaceful, Late-Night Bath

Walter Scott, novelist and poet, writing in his journal

EDINBURGH · NOVEMBER 25, 1825

I had a bad fall last night coming home. There were unfinished houses at the east end of Atholl Place, and as I was on foot, I crossed the street to avoid the material which lay about; but, deceived by the moonlight, I stepped ankle-deep in a sea of mud (honest earth and water, thank God), and fell on my hands. Never was there such a representative of Wall in Pyramus and Thisbe [Act V of Shakespeare's A Midsummer Night's Dream*]—I was absolutely rough-cast. Luckily Lady S. had retired when I came home; so I enjoyed my tub of water without either remonstrance or condolences.*

Cockburn's hospitality will get the benefit and renown of my downfall, and yet has no claim to it. In future though, I must take a coach at night—a control on one's freedom, but it must be submitted to.

∽◌∼

Sir Walter Scott was already a well-known poet when, in 1814, he published his first historical novel, *Waverley*. It was soon followed by many others and by 1825 he was, at the age of fifty-four, a wealthy and famous author, living with his wife in Edinburgh. Then a widespread financial crisis caused his publisher, Constable, to go bankrupt the following year. Scott lost much of his money.

On this November 25, Scott was walking through Edinburgh in the dark, after an evening with friends. There was no modern street lighting. It felt more like wandering in the woods, and "deceived by the moonlight, I stepped ankle-deep in a sea of mud." He reflected wryly that at least it was only "honest" mud, nothing worse: the streets were full of muck. He was even able to see the funny side, imagining himself looking like the stage character who impersonates the Wall that divides the lovers Pyramus and Thisbe in the little drama performed by the yokels in Shakespeare's *A Midsummer Night's Dream*: "I was absolutely rough-cast."

Creeping into his home, he found there was a silver lining since, by good fortune, "Lady S. had retired when I came home." His wife,

Charlotte, was already asleep. (There is a sweet affection about the name he gave her, "Lady S.," as if they laughed together at the grand title.) He could have his bath in peace, "without either remonstrance or condolences," that is, free of his wife's loving anxiety or criticism. By the time it was ready, the hour was later still. Everything was quiet.

At the end of that day, Scott "enjoyed" his bath. This little pool of warm water was the perfect antidote to what had seemed the cold "sea of mud" into which he had fallen in the darkness of the street. Regrettably, this fall would mean taking coaches in the future at night, and thus one less freedom that he must have enjoyed until now—a nighttime stroll.

But the time in the tub was simple and perfect. All his senses were now feeling better again. Letting go. Just immersed in warm water in the quiet night. Aware of all his troubles, evading nothing, knowing also the ups and downs of domestic life, he still thoroughly enjoyed the bath.

He was in fact so moved by it that he made a scene out of bathing in the novel *Count Robert of Paris* a few years later. A wounded and sickly knight is being prepared for a great battle with much care: "'Transport him instantly to a suitable apartment, only taking care that it be secret, and let him enjoy the comforts of the bath and whatever else may tend to restore his feeble animation—keeping in mind, that he must, if possible, appear tomorrow in the field.'" Scott himself was soon facing his own (financial) battle, but for this night he was restored by his own comforts of the bath.

A Long and Rewarding Life

Ptah-Hotep, scribe, completing his book of sayings

EGYPT · CA. 2400 BCE

Upon thee [the reader] many days the sun shall shine,
And length of years without default be thine.
Wisdom has caused me, in high place, to live
Long on the earth, a hundred years and ten,
I found the favour that a king can give,
First, for life's labour, honoured amongst men.

⁘

Since the late nineteenth century, the precepts of the Egyptian scribe Ptah-Hotep have been regarded as one of the oldest preserved written texts of humankind. While the dating varies, this book of sayings is certainly more than four millennia old.

The author was a high official in the Egyptian state and may well have been the man named Ptah-Hotep who was vizier at some point during the Fifth Dynasty. In his book, he gave advice on many different topics. He considered the problem of how to relate to superiors in a rigidly hierarchical society. He even discussed the best way of handling powerful people if one had received the honor of dining with them. He talked about life in marriage and the kindness between husband and wife. He praised home education. He counseled hard work, but not too much: do not waste all the daylight for the sun will set soon enough anyway.

Ptah-Hotep's circumstances were very different from ours. Some of what he said in his book now seems strange or even cruel. But there is a core of everyday experience that we can recognize. Even if the solutions have changed, some of the problems are familiar.

His own life is only visible in the background and in the choice of examples he wrote about. He must have been married from the way he talks about the life of husband and wife. He had a strong feeling for the relationship between parents and children. Perhaps at times this has tempted modern translators to make him sound too familiar, but still, he did share some of our deepest interests and concerns in life.

At the very end of this book of sayings, after all the advice had been given, Ptah-Hotep presented himself to his audience as if in common politeness. He wished his readers well in their own lives and promised prosperity for those who followed his advice. Then he reviewed his own days.

The wisdom that he had now generously shared with others had made his own life successful. He had spent it "in high place." Having been careful with his health, he had managed "to live long on the earth." Can we believe that he reached the age of 110? Perhaps like all of those who give good advice, he was tempted to exaggerate his own success in order to endorse his message! Yet the feeling is touching, whatever we decide about the actual age.

Here was a man, well over 4,000 years ago, pausing to review his own life. He was old, certainly. He had worked a lifetime. If he did have children, he would have seen them grow up. He had "found the favour" of his king, as far as that was possible. He had become "honoured amongst men." He could look back on an almost completed journey. And he did so with contentment, a touch of happiness: recognizing that it was, when almost all was said and done, a good enough life.

Here then was a man striving to come to terms with the approaching end of his days, when after the many sunrises, there would be darkness. He was realistic. He was also generous, wishing other people lives as long and fruitful as his own had been. He was able to feel happy about his own days in the sun, and so he could feel positive about other people who were to live after him. His happiness was no different from ours.

A Cottage Near the Sea

William Blake, poet and artist, writing a letter to a friend

FELPHAM, WEST SUSSEX · SEPTEMBER 23, 1800

We [Blake and his wife, Catherine] are safe arrived at our cottage without acci-dent or hindrance, though it was between eleven and twelve o'clock at night before we could get home, owing to the necessary shifting of our boxes and portfolios from one chaise to another [. . .] We travelled through a most beau-tiful country on a most glorious day. Our cottage is more beautiful than I thought it, and also more convenient, for though small it is well-proportioned, and if I should build a palace it would be only my cottage enlarged. Please to tell Mrs. Butts [the wife of his correspondent Thomas Butts] that we have dedicated a chamber for her service, and that it has a very fine view of the sea [. . .] The sweet air and the voices of winds, trees, and birds, and the odours of the happy ground, make it a dwelling for immortals. Work will go on here with Godspeed.

⊙

William Blake is now celebrated as one of the major English poets and as a distinguished artist, whose engravings illustrated his own mythological poems in a uniquely harmonious vision in two media. He was born in London's Soho area in 1757 and began his working life in around 1772 as an apprentice engraver. In 1782, he married Catherine Boucher, and they formed a close relationship that endured till his death in 1827. By the time of this letter to his dear friend Thomas Butts, he had already composed some of his best-known works, including the dual collection *Songs of Innocence and Experi-ence*. But his life was still a struggle, especially financially, and he was glad to receive the invitation of the writer William Hayley to move to a cottage arranged by Hayley in his home village on England's south coast, where the plan was for Blake to illustrate Hayley's poems while pursuing his own projects.

As a Londoner, William Blake expressed a sense almost of new birth on arriving in this rural setting, within view of the sea. The journey had been grueling. They had set off from London on Thurs-day, September 18, between six and seven in the morning, and it took them seven changes of carriage and driver to reach their cottage in the hour before midnight on Saturday the 20th. But when he wrote back to his friend in London, Blake recalled with pleasure the last day's traveling, when they began to pass through that "most beautiful country." It had been a "most glorious day," perhaps not only in weather and scenery but also in a sense of hope that he began to feel.

He had never seen the cottage before, and when he was able to view it properly, he was cheered by the same feeling of beauty that he had experienced in the surrounding countryside. To find a beautiful place to live, after the gloom of the city that he depicted in such famous poems as "London," was for Blake a source of profound well-being. His art and writing were animated by a unified vision of beauty and joy and innocence, and this new home felt like the perfect setting in which to pursue his vocation.

In the capital, he had lived his life against the grain of what he felt to be an ugly and inhumane place; now that strain was relieved. Here in Felpham, he felt, there would be harmony between his own being and the world around him instead. The "sweet air and the voices of winds, trees, and birds" were the natural complement to the world of Blake's imaginative vision. This consonance found expression in his confidence that "work will go on here with Godspeed." And indeed, he went on to compose the celebrated passage in his epic poem *Milton* about "England's green and pleasant land" in this pastoral home.

Looking ahead, the promise was not entirely to be fulfilled. He and Catherine left Felpham in 1804, after the trauma of Blake's being tried for treason (and acquitted) following a fracas with a soldier in their cottage garden at Felpham during which he had cursed both the army and the monarch at a time of intense official suspicion about revolutionary conspiracies. They felt it necessary to return to London.

Yet in this first moment of arriving at the cottage, when he seemed to have found a genuine spiritual home, the poet experienced a depth of harmony with the world around that he had not known before. It brought him a few years of great inspiration and a vision of positive being that continued to nurture his spirit in adversity. Mortality haunted Blake, but here in Felpham he found an interlude from that fear, a "dwelling for immortals."

Creativity

A Shady Grove on a Hot Day

Sappho, poet and musician, composing a lyric poem

THE ISLAND OF LESBOS · CA. EARLY SIXTH CENTURY BCE

And round about the breeze murmurs cool through apple boughs,
and slumber streams from quivering leaves.

◦◦◦

These words are the translation of a fragment of poetry that was written down over 2,500 years ago by the great poet Sappho, who was born
on the Greek island of Lesbos in the latter part of the seventh century
BCE. She lived mainly on her native island and also probably for a
time in exile in Sicily. (So she might have written this piece of poetry
while being there.) She was renowned in her life as a musician as
well, even being credited with the invention of the lyre. Images often
show her playing this instrument. Her poems were probably songs
and they were highly regarded for many centuries among the Greeks
and the Romans. But later much of Sappho's work was lost, or was
only preserved via quotations in other books. Eventually, Victorian
archaeologists rediscovered many fragments, written on papyri and
preserved in an excavated ancient rubbish heap in Egypt.

These, then, are words that have hovered on the very edge of
oblivion, recording a moment in the ancient Mediterranean, its sensations and feelings.

The day is hot. A fresh breeze whispers in a shady grove of apple
trees. It is a sleepy time when the eyes are closing in the sun. The fact
that the rest of the poem is now missing seems to turn the images back
into a very direct expression of personal experience. The moment
hangs perfectly poised between hot sun and cool breeze, consciousness and sleep. The inside and the outside world become woven
together, and sleepiness flows toward the poet from the trees. Happiness lies on the finely balanced edge where these opposites meet.
In another moment it might be over—sleep might have come or the
breeze might have died away. Such balance, making a moment perfect, cannot last beyond it.

This flash of happiness in a grove of apple trees on a hot day has been carried across the centuries by the creativity of a few words on a scrap of papyrus. It sounds improbable. Yet Sappho understood the power of her creativity. She knew her words could leap over the gaps of time. She wrote to a lover that through her words, "men, I think, will remember us even hereafter." Such creativity, springing from the momentary happiness of being alive, could not help being self-aware. While her words expressed happiness, they contained an intense awareness of both mortality and eternity.

Many centuries have passed, and countless powerful and rich individuals have vanished. Those responsible for Sappho's exile are not even a flicker in our memories. In contrast, that moment among apple trees has been preserved by her words, and with them comes the feeling of being alive in another time.

The Pleasure of Mathematical Solutions

Bhaskara, astronomer and mathematician, composing the preface to a book on numbers

UJJAIN, INDIA · CA. 1150

Having bowed to the deity [Ganesh]—whose head is like an elephant's; whose feet are adored by gods; who, when called to mind, relieves his votaries from embarrassment; and bestows happiness on his worshippers—I propound this easy process of computation: delightful by its elegance; perspicuous with words concise, soft, and correct; and pleasing to the learned.

⟡

Bhaskara was in his thirties when he wrote these verses. He was in charge of an astronomical observatory outside the ancient city of Ujjain (in today's state of Madhya Pradesh) in central India. This had been a center for mathematics and astronomy for at least five hundred years already. He was proud to be holding the same position as the mathematician whom he most admired, Brahmagupta, centuries before. Trade routes running from China connected this ancient place both to Persia and on to Europe.

Bhaskara knew that he had important things to say. The verses that follow in this and three succeeding books of his bring together algebraic and geometric ideas developed by previous Indian mathematics (responding partly to Greek predecessors) and add some new and highly sophisticated insights. Ganesh, the elephant-headed god, is the Lord of beginnings, and so he belongs in this opening moment. When Ganesh is called to mind, he carries away embarrassment, leaving us free and at ease. In doing so, he brings happiness with him.

Here, nearly a millennium ago, was a moment of happiness at the gateway leading into self-expression. Under the sign of Ganesh, all the inhibitions slipped away. Filled with confidence and assurance, the young mathematician knew where he was going.

He was ready to teach. So clear were the mathematical ideas in his mind, so prepared were the words to express them, that he was sure they would in due course bring happiness to other people. His readers would find methods for solving problems here that had previously seemed difficult, even impossible. The world would become an easier place by this "easy process of computation." Others would benefit from these teachings, as Bhaskara had benefited from the discovery of method and system, curing the obstinacy of tasks and making problems soluble. Even the learned would appreciate his instructions. This was partly a way of saying that there was something here to benefit everybody. Beginners would find that math was no longer frightening. Experts would recognize and enjoy new ideas.

Bhaskara started by explaining the rules of arithmetic, in a way that is still clear and accessible today. He expressed these ideas to Lilivati, his daughter. She represented the many readers to come. But there is also in these words the sense of a private moment of communication—a father addressed, or imagined addressing, his daughter. She shared with him in the blessings of the elephant-headed god.

It seems unlikely that everyone did find all of these mathematical ideas delightfully easy. Bhaskara was launching into unknown seas. He was the first to understand some of the difficulties involved in the idea of dividing by zero. He was the first to employ letters for unknowns in the equations of algebra. He even developed ideas about progressions and limits that in some ways resemble the theories of calculus propounded by Newton and Leibniz half a millennium later.

Yet so crystalline and "pleasing" were these concepts in Bhaskara's mind as he began to expound them that he himself saw no difficulties. The "elegance" of his ideas was expressed by words of perspicuity. He had no need to assert his personal authority or anticipate difficulties or objections. The Lord of beginnings did indeed bless this moment.

A Day among Great Thinkers

Ralph Thoresby, scholar and museum owner,
writing in his diary

LONDON · JUNE 12, 1712

Attended the Royal Society, where I found Dr. Douglas dissecting a dolphin, lately caught in the Thames, where were present the President, Sir Isaac Newton, both the Secretaries, the two Professors from Oxford (Dr. Halley and Keil), with others whose company we after enjoyed at the Grecian Coffee House. Was afterwards with Mr. Gale observing some basso-relievos at St. Paul's Church [Cathedral], particularly the six relating to the history of that apostle. And afterwards walked to the Charterhouse [. . .]; diverted ourselves in the shady walks in the wilderness there; remembered with satisfaction one of our family, Henry Thoresby, [. . .] who was so intimate with the founder [of Charterhouse] that he appointed him one of the first trustees [. . .] Was after with Mr. Gale and Mr. Oddy, a learned gentleman, at the Coffee House.

∞

Ralph Thoresby, a gentleman from Leeds in the north of England, was in London to see his many friends there. In his fifties, he was a fellow of the capital's Royal Society, at the time the premier learned and scientific body, whose president was Sir Isaac Newton. Thoresby had created a well-known museum of natural history and archaeology in his hometown and was something of an expert on Roman coins.

After conducting some business, Thoresby arrived at the Royal Society. There James Douglas was giving an anatomical demonstration, "dissecting a dolphin, lately caught in the Thames." The Society was funding Douglas to put on such shows, which brought in a bigger audience.

A number of Thoresby's friends and acquaintances were there. These were serious people, however popular the lecture. Isaac Newton was present, the man whose book *Principia Mathematica* (1687) had revealed the mechanical laws governing the universe, including the Law of Gravity. With him was Edmond Halley (who encouraged Newton to write that book and paid for its publication), himself one of the most distinguished mathematicians and astronomers of the time; and also John Keil, another Oxford professor and a defender of Newton's achievements against the claims of foreign scientist-philosophers such as Gottfried Wilhelm Leibniz.

Ralph Thoresby felt reassuringly included when his little circle adjourned to a coffeehouse "with others whose company we after enjoyed." The "Grecian" was just off Fleet Street, one of the oldest of these welcoming resorts in the city. There was a buzz of ideas, a hubbub of voices all around him. It was pure enjoyment: the atmosphere, the people, and the intellectual companionship.

From there he walked with another friend to see the sculptures at Christopher Wren's St. Paul's Cathedral, completed only recently to replace the previous building lost in the Great Fire of 1666. A new world was rising up around him. Theories and architecture, equations and art: it was a dance of new ideas.

Then he visited the Charterhouse, a London school and hospital where the latest medical ideas were being employed. Happily remembering another family connection, he returned to the coffeehouse and to more learned conversation. It had been a day alive with different voices, new perspectives opening with each encounter. He was happy to be a (small) part of it.

A Long-Sought Great Idea

Anselm of Canterbury, churchman and philosopher, writing the prologue to a theological book

ABBEY OF BEC, FRANCE · CA. 1078

I began to wonder whether perhaps it might be possible to discover just one single argument which would need nothing else to be proven beyond itself to establish that God truly exists; that there is one highest good requiring nothing else on which all things depend for their being and their flourishing; and all else that we believe about the Divine Being.

I focused my mind as often and as intensely as possible on this question and sometimes it seemed to me that I was on the point of seizing upon my object, but whenever this happened it refused to become clear in my mind. Eventually in despair I wanted to stop this pursuit of something that it seemed would never be found. But when I wanted to resist these concerns so that they should not fill my thoughts in vain to the exclusion of more practicable projects, an idea began to force itself upon me and would not be denied, however unwilling and resistant I was. When one day I was exhausted from holding out against its demands, into the strife of my thoughts there presented itself the very idea which I had despaired of attaining and I embraced it as passionately as I had resisted before.

Judge then how much I rejoiced to have found something which, if it were written out, would bring happiness also to some who read it.

❦

Anselm had been the prior at the Abbey of Bec in Normandy for over a decade, and in 1078, when he was in his forties, he became the abbot, in charge of this rich and powerful Benedictine monastery. He was destined for still greater success in the church, since he became the archbishop of Canterbury in 1093.

This passage from the prologue of Anselm's book *Proslogion* (*Proslogium*) describes what truly made him rejoice—and it was not money or power. It was something that was not even visible, something hidden deep inside his mind. Yet this passing and impalpable experience made him happy beyond his dreams.

Anselm was a great thinker as well as a successful administrator. He loved arguments and ideas. They seemed deeply real to him, more so sometimes than the material world of stones and bricks and trees. One idea in particular perplexed him and drove him on.

He wanted to find a single argument that would prove the existence and the beauty of God. But he searched not in the scriptures or the authorities of old, though he loved them, too. Instead he burrowed deep inside his own thoughts, asking himself over and over whether he could at last find his proof.

Sometimes Anselm felt on the very verge of success: "it seemed to me that I was on the point of seizing upon my object." But then his hope dissolved and the idea remained out of his mental focus. He eventually decided to abandon this intellectual search that clearly took up space that could be used for "more practicable projects." But now that he had seemingly given up, this idea, the one single argument necessary to prove the existence of God, returned to haunt him.

It is very rare indeed for a writer from the eleventh century to pick out a particular day in his own life. Yet here it is, this "one day" on which he "was exhausted from holding out." He was certainly trying to keep the issue out of his mind, feeling that he was being tormented by it. And then it burst upon him, this idea that seemed to him the crystalline, singular argument for God: God's very essence included the necessity of God's existence. In other words, since God's essence was to be supremely perfect it was inconceivable that God could *lack* any feature—such as existence—possessed by other beings.

Anselm embraced with passion this sudden great discovery, which has become famous as the ontological argument. Of course, in retrospect, not everyone has been convinced by Anselm's idea, but it is complex enough to have kept generations of both believers and skeptics fascinated. Here, before all the subtleties, he recorded that moment of joy when the idea burst into his consciousness. He was as happy as a lover in the moment of acceptance, and out of this happiness his book was born.

The Feeling of Inner Strength

Sojourner Truth, abolitionist and women's rights campaigner, telling her story to a friend

FLORENCE, MASSACHUSETTS · LATE 1840s

I'll have my child again [. . .] I have no money, but God has enough, or what's better! And I'll have my child again [. . .] Oh my God! I knew I'd have him again. I was sure God would help me to get him. Why, I felt so tall within— I felt as if the power of a nation was with me!

✺

Sojourner Truth was born around 1797 as an enslaved girl named Isabella on an estate in Ulster County, New York. She was sold successively to three owners during her childhood, the last being John Dumont and his wife, also in Ulster County. The wife in particular treated her extremely cruelly. As a young woman, Truth had been forced to marry an older slave, Thomas; she had five children. Eventually she left the Dumonts and came to stay locally with Isaac and Maria Van Wagenen. In 1827, slavery was abolished in New York State. Truth found out that her son Peter (born in about 1822) had been sent to a slaveholder called Solomon Gedney, who then sold him to a planter in Alabama. But it was illegal to sell a slave out of the state of New York.

It was about twenty years later that Sojourner Truth, who had taken this name in her subsequent career as a preacher, abolitionist, and campaigner, was telling the story of her earlier years to a friend named Olive Gilbert, whom she had met as a fellow member of the Northampton Association of Education and Industry (a utopian group) in Florence, Massachusetts. Olive Gilbert wrote down the experiences as dictated, with some comments, and they were published in 1850. It had been, in many ways, a personal conversation in which one friend told another of her life.

Here Truth reached the moment when she had gone in search of Peter and had sought out her previous owners, the Dumonts. Her aim was to find the man who had illegally sold her son.

She remembered the encounter very vividly. John Dumont's wife reacted with cruel contempt to her inquiry about Peter, and Truth recalled for Olive how she reached "a moment's hesitation" and then suddenly and irrevocably she realized that she was not going to be defeated. She knew, and was able to declare, that "I'll have my child again." This, too, was met with dismissive indifference by Dumont's wife. Where would she ever find the money to pursue her cause?

In response, Sojourner Truth found words that welled up from a deep source of inspiration inside: "I have no money, but God has enough, or what's better! And I'll have my child again." She repeated this declaration like an anthem. Later in life, she became a great orator in the cause of abolition and women's rights. As Olive Gilbert wrote, she possessed "a spirit-stirring animation" that moved her audiences. Here that stirring power of expression came to self-awareness under the pressure of a great hardship.

Many things about this encounter were deeply unhappy— Dumont's hostility and also the anguish of not yet knowing how she would recover her son. But deep inside, this was also a moment of exaltation. She later recalled that, as she heard herself speak these words of poetic beauty and assurance, she "felt so tall within." It was her own language that had given her this deep, answering self-affirmation, the happiness of discovering her own visionary will and expression. So great was the energy that she felt "as if the power of a nation was with me!"

Sojourner Truth's fight for her son's return was complicated and further testified to the force of will that she had discovered. She was directed by a friend to the home of Quakers who gave her support. From there she went to the Grand Jury at court and, with further legal help paid for by her supporters, she eventually forced the return of her young son by suing the man who had sold him illegally. Such was the threat to him—of fine and imprisonment—that Gedney had to travel to Alabama and retrieve the boy. The case was brought in the autumn of 1827, she recalled, and Peter was returned to her the following year. Her powerful words did come true: "I'll have my child again."

The Reward of Studying the Stars

Ptolemy, astronomer,
making a note in the margins of his book

ALEXANDRIA · SECOND CENTURY CE

*I know that I am mortal by nature and ephemeral, but when I trace at my plea-
sure the windings to and fro of the heavenly bodies, I no longer touch earth with
my feet. I stand in the presence of Zeus himself and take my fill of ambrosia.*

✧

Ptolemy was probably born in the late first century CE, in Egypt. He
lived and worked in the city of Alexandria during the second century
CE, and became the foremost astronomer and mathematician of the
ancient Western world. The Greeks of antiquity had developed many
aspects of what we would call pure mathematics, such as geometry.
Ptolemy was among the first to apply mathematical ideas to the real
world. He made maps; he analyzed light and music. Above all, he
watched the planets and the stars in the sky.

Ptolemy had no telescopes or other aids to enhance sight. He simply observed the night sky as it grew dark outside the city. He had his
own way of recording these observations and he also used records
going back, in some cases, for centuries. The thirteen sections of his
book *The Mathematical Compilation* became the most important influence for many thinkers on concepts about the solar system and the
universe beyond—until the heliocentric understanding developed
during the Renaissance. So great was its status that the book was generally known as *Almagest*, from both the Greek and the Arabic for
"greatest," making it "the greatest book."

While the scientific authority of Ptolemy's astronomical records
was ultimately superseded, they still offer us the extraordinary sense
of a man looking up at the "heavenly bodies" at precise moments
that passed nearly two millennia ago. Because his records are so
detailed, we know that Ptolemy made his first observation on the day
that we would call March 26 in the year 127 CE. His final observation
of the planets and stars was noted down on February 2 in the year 141
CE. During those fourteen years, we can trace his nights of viewing

when he made treasured observations about the movement of particular bodies. There was, for example, an early morning in February of 134 CE when he saw Venus, and an evening in February of 140 CE when the same planet came into his view.

An interesting controversy has long surrounded some of these records. It appears that Ptolemy adjusted some of his collected data so that his complex mathematical model could be fittingly applied. Critics have accused him of cheating. But in reality, he was doing what great theorists have always needed to do: balancing the messiness of the real world with the perfection of the abstract model. He was not interested simply in more and more data but in coming to understand the patterns behind the countless details.

Near the beginning of his book, Ptolemy made a note of how he felt. He knew that he was "mortal by nature and ephemeral." Yet when he looked up at the heavens and saw the stars, he was lifted out of his ordinary mortal condition for a moment. And it was not simply what he saw that made Ptolemy happy. It was the sense that he understood "the windings to and fro" of the stars and planets. Through his theories, he found order in the apparent randomness of the universe.

That was why on such nights, Ptolemy felt as if he was standing by the side of Zeus, sharing heavenly nectar. This happiness was an inseparable and integral part of his achievement. Why else would a man have stood night after night in darkness, pursuing his solitary quest for knowledge, waiting for the skies to reveal their secret?

The Longing to Write

Francesco Petrarca, poet and scholar, writing a letter to a friend

FONTAINE-DE-VAUCLUSE, FRANCE · CA. 1340

Strangely enough I long to write, but do not know what or to whom. This inexorable passion has such a hold upon me that pen, ink, and paper and work prolonged far into the night, are more to my liking than repose and sleep. In short, I find myself always in a sad and languishing state when I am not writing, and, anomalous though it seems, I labour when I rest, and find my rest in labour. My mind is hard as rock, and you might well think that it really sprang from one of Deucalion's stones [Greek myth of stones that turned into people].

Let this tireless spirit pore eagerly over the parchment, until it has exhausted both fingers and eyes by the long strain, yet it feels neither heat nor cold, but would seem to be reclining upon the softest down. It is only fearful that it may be dragged away, and holds fast the mutinous members [. . .] My mind finds itself refreshed by prolonged exercise, as the beast of burden by his food and rest. What then am I to do, since I cannot stop writing, or bear even the thought of rest? I write to you, not because what I have to say touches you nearly, but because there is no one so accessible just now who is at the same time so eager for news, especially about me, and so intelligently interested in strange and mysterious phenomena, and ready to investigate them.

⁓⊷⊷⊷⁓

In his mid-thirties, Francesco Petrarca was achieving fame as a scholar and author when he wrote to the abbot Peter of St. Benigno in Italy about his passion for writing. It was around the year 1340 and he was probably at his home in Fontaine-de-Vaucluse in southern France. He had been working on an epic poem called *Africa* (about Roman history), his poetry was acclaimed throughout learned Europe, and honors accumulated: in 1340 he received invitations from both Paris and Rome to be crowned as poet laureate in imitation of ceremonies performed in ancient Rome. He agreed to be crowned on the Capitoline Hill in the Eternal City. But the real motive for his writing did not lie in such public recognition. On the contrary, the true fulfillment of being a writer came to him in his secluded study when he was all by himself.

As he sat down to begin this letter, Petrarca noticed that he felt an "inexorable passion" when he had "pen, ink, and paper" at hand. He needed to write, no matter if he had anyone to write to or not. There is a wry self-knowledge in these words, as he acknowledged to the abbot that he was really writing for its own sake and not so much to address anyone in particular. He simply loved the business of writing more than anything else in the world.

Petrarca's words also expressed his pleasure in the physical act of writing. He liked the feel of the pen in his fingers and the look of the paper as he put word after word in ink on it.

All times of day were good for writing but it seems to have been best of all when he wrote "far into the night," which brought a deep peace to his soul, a tranquillity happier than any sleep. It was as if the more energy he used, the more energetic he felt, "refreshed by prolonged exercise." The harder he wrote, the more he was in love with the physical experience of covering the pages: "Let this tireless spirit pore eagerly over the parchment, until it has exhausted both fingers and eyes." As he moved those aching fingers over the page, he felt a sense of supreme fulfillment. This was his calling.

Paternal Praise for a First Novel

Fanny Burney, novelist, writing in her journal

CHESSINGTON, SURREY · JUNE 18, 1778

I received from Charlotte [Fanny's sister] a letter, the most interesting that could be written to me, for it acquainted me that dear father was, at length, reading my book, which has now been published six months.

How this has come to pass, I am yet in the dark; but, it seems, that the very moment almost that my mother [Fanny's stepmother, Elizabeth] and Susan and Sally [Fanny's sister Susanna and half-sister, Sarah] left the house, he desired Charlotte to bring him the Monthly Review; *she contrived to look over his shoulder as he opened it, which he did at the account of* Evelina *[. . .] He read it with great earnestness, then put it down; and presently after snatched it up, and read it again. Doubtless, his paternal heart felt some agitation for his girl, in reading a review of her publication! How he got at the name, I cannot imagine. Soon after he turned to Charlotte, and bidding her come close to him, he put his finger on the word "Evelina," and [. . .] bade her write down the name, and send the man to Lowndes [publisher of* Evelina], *as if for herself. This she did, and away went William [. . .]*

But the next day I had a letter from Susan, in which I heard that he had begun reading it with Lady Hales [. . .] Susan begged to have, then, my father's real and final opinion; and it is such that I almost blush to write, even for my own private reading; but yet is such as I can by no means suffer to pass unrecorded, as my whole journal contains nothing so grateful to me. I will copy his own words, according to Susan's solemn declaration of their authenticity: "Upon my word I think it the best novel I know, except Fielding's, and, in some respects, better than his!"

⬳∞⬲

Fanny Burney had just turned twenty-six. Her father was the renowned English musician Charles Burney. On this June day in 1778, she was staying with a family friend, Samuel Crisp, at his home outside London. She had just received important news from her family home back in the city.

Six months ago, Fanny Burney had published her first book, a novel titled *Evelina: Or the History of A Young Lady's Entrance into the World*. It had been very well received. In accordance with the customs of her time, being a young lady, she had not put her name on the cover. Since she had also concealed from her father the fact that she had been writing it, she thought her authorship was hidden from him. Her brother and her sisters did know the secret. And now her father had realized the truth.

The first sign had been when her sister Charlotte had found their father reading a review of the novel. He was deeply focused. Then he asked Charlotte to arrange for the purchase of a copy, and to pretend that the book was "for herself." He sounded very solemn. Was there going to be trouble about *Evelina* with Charles Burney?

He took the novel off to read with a friend, Lady Hales. This must have produced some suspense in the household while the siblings were waiting for him to comment. Then Susan had "begged to have [. . .] father's real and final opinion." At this point in her record, Fanny Burney's feelings broke into her narrative as she recorded how "it is such that I almost blush to write, even for my own private reading." The news had been good. It made her very happy to think of it.

Instead of disapproving or being critical, her father had declared that "'Upon my word I think it is the best novel I know.'" He compared it to the work of Henry Fielding, one of the most celebrated writers at this time. He even believed it was "in some respects, better than his."

When she read these words in Susan's letter, and imagined him saying it, Fanny Burney experienced a moment of self-confirmation so joyful that "my whole journal contains nothing so grateful to me." It flowed through her, this new assurance. Her creative self was now out in the sunlight at last.

She had had a struggle over her writing. Her stepmother had tried to stop her even keeping a private journal. Now she was confident and ready to move forward. Fanny Burney went on to become a successful and celebrated novelist, whose stories are read to this day.

The Lightning Flash of Knowledge

Benjamin Franklin, scientist and statesman,
writing a letter to a friend

PHILADELPHIA · OCTOBER 31, 1751

I forget whether I wrote to you [Cadwallader Colden, a fellow scientist] that I have melted brass pins and steel needles, inverted the poles of the magnetic needle, given a magnetism and polarity to needles that had none, and fired dry gunpowder by the electric spark. I have five bottles that contain eight or nine gallons each, two of which charged are sufficient for those purposes; but I can charge and discharge them altogether. There are no bounds (but what expense and labour give) to the force man may raise and use in the electrical way; for bottle may be added to bottle in infinitum and all united and discharged together as one, the force and effect proportioned to their number and size. The greatest known effects of common lightning may, I think, without much difficulty, be exceeded in this way, which a few years since could not have been believed, and even now may seem to many a little extravagant to suppose. So we are got beyond the skill of Rabelais' [sixteenth-century French author] devils of two years old, who, he humorously says, had only learnt to thunder and lighten a little round the head of a cabbage.

Benjamin Franklin was in his mid-forties when he performed the experiments that he described in this letter to a scientific friend. He had achieved financial security through his printing business and through publishing and writing, including his highly popular *Poor Richard's Almanack*. Now retired and with the status of a gentleman, he was free to pursue his scientific researches.

Here he was trying out ways of generating and using electrical sparks. This was more the enthusiasm and ingenuity of the inventor at work than the seriousness and prudence of the statesman he was to become in the coming struggle for American independence from Britain. He was enjoying life among the bottles and the needles that were scattered around him.

Every detail of this account expressed his delight in the ingenuity of his own devices; the bottles with their electrical fluid excited him like birthday presents. He was fascinated by the range of effects he could produce, the melting of metal and the shifting patterns of magnetism. A new physical world was opening up to him and his passionate interest overflowed in the rush of these magician-like powers.

Then there followed a moment of deepening realization that there would be "no bounds" to the powers of this new force, except for the limitations of human industry and resources. He brushed aside "the greatest known effects" of natural, "common lightning" in a sweeping moment of happy confidence. It was not merely personal confidence, though, but belief in human creativity as a whole. What he was doing with these bits and bobs would carry forward in the hands of others into a great legacy.

For better or worse, a new relationship was dawning between humanity and nature. Yet this moment of realization was also full of playfulness. Franklin found himself reminded of some infantile demons imagined by the French satirist Rabelais. They have only just begun to acquire their magic powers and all they can do is crackle and flash "a little round the head of a cabbage." In these words, the pleasure of ingenious invention and the excitement of learning spilled over into humor.

Benjamin Franklin must have been pleased to think that he was about to give society this new knowledge. As he fiddled with the new gadgets and thought of the flashes brighter than common lightning in the sky, he was of course feeling confident. But there was a genuine humility at the core of his sense of achievement. Other people would follow who would truly comprehend what he was just starting to see. He rejoiced that humanity showed such promise of greater invention and understanding.

The Vitality of Spring

Edward FitzGerald, poet and translator,
writing a letter to a friend

BOULGE, SUFFOLK · APRIL 21, 1837

Ah! I wish you were here to walk with me now that the warm weather is come at last. Things have been delayed but to be more welcome, and to burst forth twice as thick and beautiful. This is boasting however, and counting of the chickens before they are hatched: the East winds may again plunge us back into winter; but the sunshine of this morning fills one's pores with jollity, as if one had taken laughing gas. Then my house is getting on: the books are up in the bookshelves and do my heart good; then Stothard's Canterbury Pilgrims [Thomas Stothard's etchings of Chaucer's characters] are over the fireplace; Shakespeare in a recess: how I wish you were here for a day or two!

༄

Edward FitzGerald was furnishing a cottage in the grounds of his parents' grand house in the hamlet of Boulge, near the town of Woodbridge in East Anglia. He was in his late twenties, and his correspondent John Allen was a close friend from their time as students at Cambridge University a few years prior. Allen was already becoming an eminent clergyman, while FitzGerald had yet to find his vocation. Meanwhile he was reading poetry in several languages. He would later become famous through his English version of the Persian poem "The Rubaiyat" by Omar Khayyam (1048–1131). FitzGerald's translation was originally published anonymously in 1859 and achieved success over the next decade, until he eventually acknowledged its authorship.

On this April day in 1837, he felt life "burst forth," exploding into flower, after a long wait. Suddenly, the world seemed to have a lot more in it, "thick and beautiful." Spring was lovely, partly because there was simply more vitality present now. It was as if each moment contained more life than whole days during winter. For FitzGerald that day, the beauty of spring was not mere prettiness. The new season was coming all in a rush, like a force being unleashed.

Every kind of beginning was wrapped up together in this "jollity." His new home, all the bustle and preparation, were caught up in this new energy. Normally rather reserved and somber, FitzGerald was all the more conscious of the bubbling-up happiness that was upon him now, "as if one had taken laughing gas" (a relatively recent discovery). It felt as if some laughing spirit was taking hold of him. There was even a certain sense of exciting danger, as if the pleasure were too great, as if he might be saturated by such an intense sensation. It had a narcotic power.

FitzGerald did not easily feel happy, which was perhaps one reason for this subtle edge of risk and even fear. Yet when a moment of happiness came, he was all the more aware of it. Happiness seemed to enter his soul from outside. He felt it as a free gift, a blessing come upon him. His fearful nature still talked to him of counting chickens too soon. He knew that the minute he started to enjoy the spring warmth, he could be plunged into a renewed chill. Yet he was too cheered to give in to his darker side. His joyfulness overrode his innate nervousness.

Back in his cottage, the books themselves seemed full of encouragement, now that they were up on their shelves. When the air was full of vigor outside in the lanes and fields, then in his heart it felt good to see the *Canterbury Pilgrims* above the fireplace, and Shakespeare in the alcove, like the patron saint of literature itself on this joyful day.

In his later comments on Omar Khayyam, Edward FitzGerald praised the way of falling "back upon Today (which has outlasted so many Tomorrows!) as the only Ground he got to stand upon, however momentarily slipping from under his Feet." On that sunny Suffolk morning, he himself had learned the same lesson as he appreciated the richness of the passing hour. Like Chaucer's pilgrims on their road to Canterbury, he still had a long journey to travel, but on such a lovely spring day he could feel that both the energy of the natural world and the literary tradition were ready to offer their support to his own creative powers.

Love

The Best Perfume

Elizabeth Barrett, poet,
writing a letter to her betrothed

LONDON · DECEMBER 1845

I have put some of [your] hair into a little locket which was given to me when I was a child by my favourite uncle, Papa's only brother, who used to tell me that he loved me better than my own father did, and was jealous when I was not glad. It is through him in part, that I am richer than my sisters—through him and his mother—and a great grief it was and trial, when he died a few years ago in Jamaica, proving by his last act that I was unforgotten. And now I remember how he once said to me: "Do you beware of ever loving! If you do, you will not do it half: it will be for life and death."

So I put the hair into his locket, which I wear habitually, and which never had hair before—the natural use of it being for perfume—and this is the best perfume for all hours, besides the completing of a prophecy.

⸝⸜∞⸝⸜

Elizabeth Barrett had first met Robert Browning when he visited her at her home in the center of London seven months before this letter. She was in her late thirties, an invalid who rarely left her bedroom in the London family house. She was already a well-known poet, as indeed was her visitor. He had made contact initially in a letter expressing his admiration for her work.

Their friendship soon deepened into love. This was all kept secret because of the domestic despotism of her father, Edward Moulton Barrett. The exchange of little tokens was like smuggled contraband, romance and adventure blended into a delicious elixir.

Whenever her brothers or sisters got married, their father denied them his consent and then promptly disinherited them. That was why the modest inheritance Elizabeth Barrett had from her uncle was important—and why she referred to it in this romantic letter to Browning. This financial security was the basis of the plan they were devising: to marry secretly and then flee to Italy. Without this money, their scheme would have been merely a game of fantasizing.

So this was a letter of reassurance: they would have enough to get to Italy together. (They did indeed marry and move to Tuscany the following year.) Then she obviously felt she could be less practical and tell Browning the story of her uncle's prophecy—that once she was in love, it would be forever. She would never recover and "'it will be for life and death.'" The words were her pledge to her lover, an anecdotal declaration of faith.

She had also been given a plainer present by her uncle, a little treasure to remember him by, a locket that she always wore in his memory. She had kept a drop of perfume in it, perhaps as a restorative on her many days of ill health.

Now she enclosed there safely a lock of Robert Browning's hair. As she told him her secret, she might have lifted the locket to her lips; she felt that this little token was "the best perfume for all hours." It was the scent of sweet freedom and love, the soft trace of their future in the heavy air of her semi-captivity in London. She was happy now as she realized this was already fulfilling her uncle's prophecy: Her first love would be forever.

A Thousand Kisses

Honoré de Balzac, novelist,
writing a letter to his beloved

PARIS · OCTOBER 28, 1833

I went to bed at two o'clock, after having walked home through the deserted silent streets of the Luxembourg quarter, admiring the blue sky, the effects of moonlight and mist on the Luxembourg, the Pantheon, Saint Sulpice, the Val de Grace, the Observatory, and the boulevards, drowned in torrents of thought, and carrying about me two notes for a thousand francs each! But I no longer bestowed a thought on them. It was my valet who found them. That lovely night had plunged me into ecstasy; you were in the skies! They spoke to me of love; I walked on listening to find out whether your dear voice might not fall from those stars, sweet and harmonious on my ears, and vibrate in my heart; and my idol, my flower, my life, I embroidered some arabesques on the wretched frame of my days of sorrow and labour.

[. . .] I am back in my study, correcting proofs, recovered from my excursions into the world of matter of fact, again taking up my chimeras, my loves; and going to bed at six in the evening, my frugality, and my bodily inactivity, will be resumed.

Goodbye till tomorrow, my love; I shall get up at midnight on Friday morning, in short, and I shall begin by reading over again your last letter to see whether I have not forgotten to answer you in any point.

We have had here for the last week a real summer, the loveliest weather in creation. Paris is superb. Love of my life, a thousand kisses are confided to the air for you, a thousand thoughts of happiness scattered during my wanderings, and an unspeakable disdain at the sight of men.

❦

Honoré de Balzac was a busy man. He spent his nights writing his novels ("I shall get up at midnight"), which were already bringing success and would soon make him one of the most celebrated French authors of the nineteenth century. He lived mostly by a severe and focused routine, driven to compose his stories in lonely concentration.

But recently he had had a life-changing encounter with the woman to whom he was writing this letter, the Polish countess Evelina Hanska.

In 1832—Balzac was in his early thirties—she had written to him to express her admiration for one of his books. She was married to a wealthy nobleman, but she had come to Switzerland in September of 1833, a few weeks before this letter, to meet Balzac at Neuchâtel. They had fallen in love and then she had to go home.

But this was not a letter of sadness or separation. He was describing a deeply positive experience. Last night, he had been walking home through the streets of Paris. It had already been a pleasant sight, "admiring the blue sky, the effects of moonlight and mist" on the great buildings of the city. At the same time, he was preoccupied with his feelings, "drowned in torrents of thought." He was so swept up by his love that he was carrying with him "two notes for a thousand francs each" and then forgot about them—even though money was important to him.

Then the night was magically transfigured. Suddenly Balzac felt as if his lover's presence was all around him, as if indeed she "were in the skies!" Instead of being far away, she appeared to be an immediate presence. She had become his whole world.

So intense was this feeling that he even hoped he might hear her "dear voice" right there. This was a moment of complete ecstasy: distance became closeness, anxiety turned into assurance. They would never be apart now. They were always going to be close. She would be with him always and everywhere. In fact, it took many years before they were to marry, long after her husband had died and only shortly before Balzac's own death.

Yet whatever that future, this was a moment when love itself became a simple sensation of happiness. Beyond even the touch and sight of the beloved, love was everything.

Then Balzac was back in his ordinary routine. But it was suffused by the glow of that moment.

The Harmony of Souls

John Smith, businessman,
writing in his journal

BURLINGTON, NEW JERSEY · MAY 26, 1748

Was at [a Quaker] meeting [. . .] This was to me a peculiarly good meeting. I waited in it for a sense whether it would be suitable for me to renew my visits to dear Hannah Logan; and in my waiting my mind was filled with sweetness, and enlarged in pure love and a particular openness and freedom, so that I determined in the affirmative [. . .]

In the evening I rode to Stenton. Hannah and her mother were not at home, but soon came, and my dearest Creature received me with a decent agreeable freedom, and we conversed together with solid delight and pleasure [. . .]

Had my dear Hannah's company several hours, and received the fullest assurances of a reciprocal love and tenderness. Our conversation was in boundless confidence, and with the most perfect harmony our souls seemed entirely knit and united together, and we jointly breathed that the Eternal One might bless us in a sacred and indissoluble tie, and might make us one another's joy in him.

⟡

John Smith was a capable young man who was already successful in the banking business. He was born and lived in the town of Burlington, New Jersey, not far from Philadelphia. In his mid-twenties, he had known Hannah Logan for some time and they had seemed to be getting on well. He liked her. But then they had become less at ease together, perhaps because his intentions were becoming more serious. He had not seen her for a while now.

Hannah Logan was slightly younger than John Smith. She was the daughter of James Logan, previously secretary to William Penn (the founder of Pennsylvania) and now a wealthy statesman of the colony. Smith's own family was doing well, but perhaps the Logans' status also made him nervous of Hannah. That day in May, though, he wanted to see her again.

In his uncertainty, John Smith went and sat in a Quaker meeting and waited to feel an inner sign. Should he take the risk of visiting her—or would it be better to wait?

In the calm of the meeting, with its reflective sharing of silence, he did become aware of his inner self. He found that his "mind was filled with sweetness," as all the hesitation naturally resolved into a sense of purpose. His inner world seemed to expand. The horizons stretched. His mind was suffused with the happiness of being in love and he was now certain. He would go and see Hannah Logan later that day.

First, he had friends over for lunch. Then he rode to Stenton, the Philadelphia country home of the Logan family. Hannah was out but he decided to wait. He was not giving in now, although it would have been a perfect excuse to leave it all for another time.

Soon enough Hannah Logan and her mother came home. How would she treat him? He has a lovely expression to describe her welcome: "Hannah [. . .] received me with a decent agreeable free-dom"—modest, as required by society, and yet friendly, too. At the same time, it was in tune with his own hopeful burst of "openness and freedom." Despite all the restraint of their manners and values, this was a moment of liberation, the coming of inner and outer freedom.

He was pleased and relieved, too, as they "conversed together with solid delight and pleasure." Now there was none of the strain that had inhibited them when last they met. The longer they talked, the happier this moment of true communication became. Their conversation was of "boundless confidence," and "reciprocal love and tenderness" pointed their way to a future together.

The world became full of space and promise. The boundaries separating them apparently dissolved and they felt "the most perfect harmony" of souls.

A Tingling about the Heart

Sydney Owenson, novelist,
writing a letter to her fiancé

DUBLIN · OCTOBER 31, 1811

I am not half such a little rascal as you suppose; the best feelings only have detained me from you; and feelings better than the best will bring me back to you. I must be more or less than woman to resist tenderness, goodness, excellence, like yours, and I am simply woman, aye, dear, "every inch a woman." I feel a little kind of tingling about the heart, at once more feeling myself nestled in yours; do you remember? Well, dear, if you don't, I will soon revive your recollection. I said I would not write to you today, but I could not resist it, and I am now going off to a man of business, and about Lady Abercorn's books, in the midst of the snow, and pinched with cold. God bless you, love.

⁓

Sydney Owenson was already a successful poet, and also a rising novelist, by 1811. She was still young, probably in her mid-twenties (though as she refused to reveal her exact year of birth, her age remains uncertain). She was the daughter of an Irish actor, educated by her mother in Dublin, and very much a self-made success. Presently, she was the companion to the aristocratic Lady Abercorn, whose physician was Thomas Charles Morgan—to whom Owenson wrote this letter. They were recently engaged and would marry the next year.

She began by referring to herself as "not half such a little rascal," which hinted at the intimate language of their relationship. It was also a hint of something else, her own height being under four feet, which she evidently turned to advantage by creating this persona full of self-mockery and humor. Morgan's own small stature had been one reason why Lady Abercorn had introduced them to each other, and so these words carry in them the playful response of the couple to other people's view of them.

Sydney Owenson was able to express intimate feeling with great delicacy but also directness, suggesting how she and her fiancé must have been developing a deep mutual understanding. She felt, she said, a "tingling about the heart" at the thought of being close to him. It was both the memory of a happy time and a happy feeling in itself. That tingling was the sensation of being loved and in love, the closing of the circle like the closing of the arms round her. It was security and stability after a long and self-possessed journey from poverty and exclusion.

The memory of that moment of closeness was sustaining and she saw the letter as another form of embrace, a kind of closeness achieved through writing. It was as if she wanted to prevent any gap from opening between them. Meanwhile, she was busy with Lady Abercorn's business in the world outside. The snow-covered streets were the opposite of the warm and tingling embrace of intimacy. They must have made the happiness seem even more vivid and glowing.

A Skeptic Has Lost His Head

Leo Tolstoy, young aristocrat and future novelist, writing in his diary

MOSCOW · JANUARY 25, 1851

I have fallen in love, or imagine myself to have fallen in love. It happened at an evening party.

I quite lost my head. I have bought a horse which I do not need.

Rules—Never to offer anything for that which I do not require. On arriving at a ball, to invite some lady to dance and to take with her one turn in a polka or a waltz.

This evening I must think out ways and means, and set my affairs in order. Meanwhile, stay at home.

⁘

Leo Tolstoy was twenty-three, the son of aristocratic Russian land-owners. He had lost his parents while still a child and had been brought up by two aunts, successively. His student days had been unsettled and unhappy. Now he was living in Moscow, plunging into the wealthy social life there. He was already in debt, usually bored, and still uncertain about the future.

On a January evening, he had gone to yet another party. He had not expected anything special, only the usual distractions from his inner unhappiness. Instead, something extraordinary occurred. It was like a thunderbolt in a clear sky when he found: "I have fallen in love." (Apparently she was a married princess.) He had not set out to find love that evening. He disapproved of these parties, though he could not resist attending. His previous relationships had been superficial. But suddenly the feeling had found him, amid all his introspection.

Tolstoy's immediate response was the typically skeptical doubt that he might only "imagine myself to have fallen in love." Yet even his doubts were full of freshness. Nor did they last at all, since he passed instantly on to record how "it happened at an evening party." The impact of love was too strong to be merely imaginary, though it might have had some imagination mixed in with it. Did he just have a crush? Or was this a deeper emotion?

The experience did sweep him off his feet: "I quite lost my head." It was such a sudden sensation and so powerful, unlike his tepid feelings at the time. His happiness expressed itself soon afterwards in a gift to himself, absurd and carefree: "I have bought a horse." His skeptical self pointed out that he did not need a horse. But the joy persisted. His old inhibitions had been broken. He was free to buy a horse, if he wished to do so. Happiness permitted it.

It was a totally liberating feeling. Now he was simply a young man in love, not a restless, dissatisfied aristocrat.

He began to fight against this sudden liberation and spoke of imposing new "rules," such as "Never to offer anything for that which I do not require." But it was too late. There was no great future to this amour, as events transpired. Instead of romance, it was war that called Tolstoy, and he soon enlisted in the Imperial Russian Army. Yet that feeling of love was complete as it was. Even if fleeting, happiness had struck.

Venus Kept Her Promise

Sulpicia, young noblewoman, composing a lyric poem

ROME · CA. 30 BCE

At last love has come—and such a love that
I would be more ashamed to have it hidden than revealed.
Venus, won over by my muses, brought him
And dropped him in my lap.
She kept her word. Now let my happiness speak
For itself and others if they have not had their own.

⌦

Sulpicia lived during the reign of Emperor Augustus. She was the daughter of a senator and the niece of an even more powerful Roman statesman. We know little about her, and only half a dozen of her poems have survived. But they do speak very directly of her personal life. A theme running through the poems that we have is a relationship outside marriage. Here, the young man—to whom she gives the name Cerinthus—had just come into her life.

She had waited a long time for love to come. She had devoted her muse, her poetry, to making the goddess Venus favorable. How many poems and pleas did it take to win such favor? At last the reward for all her devotion and persistence had arrived. Since Venus had kept her promise, it would be folly to renounce what she was offering.

Of course Sulpicia writes in the manner of a remote period, playing with religious and mythological ideas just as the male poets of the time did. But the words also record an actual moment when happiness broke into a particular woman's life and she decided to seize it—and her lover.

It was like receiving a sudden present, the abrupt entry of this young man into her world. Venus had "brought him and dropped him in my lap." It was as if one moment Sulpicia's arms were empty and the next, there he was clasped in her embrace. Her contemporary, the poet Horace, advised his followers to "seize the moment." Otherwise happiness would simply pass us by. So she seized her moment and with it, this young man. Before it was too late and he got away.

Roman women were brought up to be modest. Yet Sulpicia felt at that moment like shouting the news from the rooftops. When happiness was so freely given by the gods, it would be more of a sin to conceal it than to let it be known. It would be ungrateful to Venus not to tell everyone how well she had kept her promise. For her as a poet, the words were part of the feeling: being happy and expressing it this way composed one complete experience.

Sulpicia imagined the reaction. She knew very well how people were going to talk about her. They would say it was shameful, doubly shameful: first the deed and then the confession. But that was only because they themselves had never known such an overwhelming experience of happiness.

A Matchless Face

Richardson Pack, army officer, writing a poem

- ABERDEEN · OCTOBER 26, 1728

When first I saw you (who says Love is blind?)
Your bending Head was on your Arm reclin'd;
A down-cast Look, but yet superior Grace
Adorn'd with modest Airs your matchless Face.

⟨∞⟩

Richardson Pack was in his late forties. He had had a successful career as a British army officer from which he had been retired prosperously in East Anglia. Then, after years of peaceful retirement, he was called to rejoin his former regiment, initially at Exeter in southwest England. From there they marched to Aberdeen in the far northeast of Scotland, as part of King George II's campaigns against Jacobite rebels that continued over many years after the unsuccessful rising of 1715. Major Pack had distinguished himself in his earlier career, notably in 1710 when fighting in Spain. Now, however, he was unprepared for the rigors of garrisoning cold northern towns and he died of a fever in Aberdeen in December 1728. These lines of poetry belonged to his very final months.

He was unhappily married, and so these words were not written to his wife but to a woman he called Clara; her true name is unknown. The poem as a whole was published in a posthumous collection, but it had been written as if it were personally addressed to Clara—even if it was never to be presented to her. These four lines were the vividly imagined and deeply felt opening of the entire poem.

His words expressed the memory of a happy moment, revived in a difficult situation. He was now far from home and finding himself a soldier once more, after he had finally been able to retire and settle down. He was in danger again, involved in an armed conflict. He must have sensed this destiny wrapping round his life in Aberdeen, a granite city on a stormy sea. He was too old for this now and so, turning his mind back, he longed for the good days when he had been at peace.

One of the best moments must have been "when first I saw you." Now, talking to Clara in his imagination, made the original scene as immediate as it had once been.

It was more of a vision than a simple memory, as if Clara were right in front of him: her graceful form, her "bending Head" resting on her arm. As he imagined to write to her now, the feeling of that first glimpse returned, with all the original charm of the casual gesture of her head "on your Arm reclin'd." She had been relaxed yet beautifully balanced, like a classical sculpture.

Then there had been her "down-cast Look." She was not meeting his eyes and perhaps she was a little somber or just serious. She might have been shy and yet her presence was overwhelming. Now he felt again the upsurge of joy when he had first sensed her "superior Grace" and seen her "matchless Face."

He was not really a poet, but he had skill enough to convey the feeling of that moment when life felt worthwhile because of the sight of Clara's peerless face. It was an instant when the world revealed what beauty it had to show.

Now, in this faraway, northern city and drawn into a fight that would soon lead to his death, the moment floated into Richardson Pack's thought like a warm breeze from another world.

The Softness of His Lips

Mary Wollstonecraft, novelist and philosopher,
writing a letter to her lover

PARIS · DECEMBER 1793

Recollection now makes my heart bound to thee; but, it is not to thy money-getting face, though I cannot be seriously displeased with the exertion which increases my esteem, or rather is what I should have expected from thy character.—No; I have thy honest countenance before me—Pop—relaxed by tenderness; a little—little wounded by my whims; and thy eyes glistening with sympathy.—Thy lips then feel softer than soft—and I rest my cheek on thine, forgetting all the world.—I have not left the hue of love out of the picture—the rosy glow; and fancy has spread it over my own cheeks, I believe, for I feel them burning, whilst a delicious tear trembles in my eye, that would be all your own, if a grateful emotion directed to the Father of nature, who has made me thus alive to happiness, did not give more warmth to the sentiment it divides—I must pause a moment.

Need I tell you that I am tranquil after writing thus?

⸎

Mary Wollstonecraft was in her mid-thirties when she came from London to live in the revolutionary Paris of the early 1790s. It was an extraordinary place, where the greatest monarchy of eighteenth-century Europe had been overthrown by an uprising that was itself increasingly divided and uneasy. In this ferment, she had written a book that soon made her a notable author: a radical argument entitled *A Vindication of the Rights of Woman.*

Moving in circles frequented by supporters of the Girondists (the more moderate revolutionary faction), she had met the American Gilbert Imlay. He had been a soldier in the American Revolution and had now come to Europe, attracted partly by the upheaval and also by the hope of making his fortune. Imlay was handsome, charming—and untrustworthy. Their relationship was not destined to be lasting or happy. In 1794, she gave birth to their daughter, but as relations broke down, she attempted suicide in 1795. Nevertheless, it was (on

191

its own terms) a passionate time, and it revealed new horizons in life for Wollstonecraft.

In this letter, written while Imlay was away on business, she tried to express the essence of this experience. She focused her mind on his presence. His face was more vividly impressed on her consciousness than an ordinary memory: it was a moment of immediate connection, as if her love was there, right then. This "makes my heart bound to thee," she wrote. She felt very close to him, as if locked in an embrace that would never be broken.

He was away working on another scheme to make money, and Wollstonecraft drew a slightly sharp contrast between his worldly self and his "honest countenance." She knew he was not really someone to be trusted. A current of anxiety was already here, but that other face, the loving expression, was stronger for now—it was as if he were gazing back at her, as if he were present.

His image had entered her thoughts with a soft and sudden "Pop," as if by magic. This little flash of humor seemed to set her at ease as she wrote. She saw him "relaxed by tenderness"—no doubt, he, too, was in love. She set aside her knowledge of his "money-getting face," feeling his more generous self emerge in her thoughts.

The moment was not perfect because there was still a shadow. She was aware that he was hurt by some conflict, which she tactfully saw now as caused by her own "whims." But all was set right by the look of his eyes, "glistening with sympathy." That was the source of her joy: the light in Gilbert Imlay's eyes, a glowing look of love.

All of her emotions became one united instant in the kiss, the sensation of his lips, the touch both then and renewed in recollection. She was absorbed by the pleasure of this softness. There was also in this kiss the promise that they would once again be together.

The soft meeting of lips made for Mary Wollstonecraft a moment of love that was outside the passing of time. The kiss, in her present imagination and as experienced in the past, subsided gently into the peace of simply being together with "my cheek on thine." She was grateful both to him and to the divine power in life itself, even if she could not forget the tensions in their relationship. She embraced the kiss and rejoiced in being "alive to happiness."

A Comfortable Moment of Communion

Claire de Rémusat, companion to Empress Josephine,
writing a letter to her husband

*I am vexed at the length of your absence. Three weeks more before I shall see
you! This is a long and wearisome separation. You cannot picture to yourself
how I grieve about it. It was long since we had been parted, and the delightful
habit of being with you had regained its old influence over me. Each day I feel
your companionship more necessary. I think that our minds are more than
ever in unison, that our opinions are more often the same, and that we know
all the charm of union. In youth, a diversity of tastes and opinions, which at
that time is more strongly felt, does no harm to love, and indeed contributes to
it, by affording opportunities of self-sacrifice; but when years have crept upon
us, quieter and safer joys become preferable, and harmony and unity are then
our best happiness.*

*You will admit, this time, that I am writing for the pleasure of writing, and
truly there is nothing in Paris for me to tell you, not even in my own little
circle. I am lazily lying in bed; the weather is cold; I have not the least inclination to go out, and find myself very comfortable, with my desk on my knees,
writing to you all that comes into my head, or rather my heart.*

⋘⋙

Claire de Rémusat was thirty years old, married for more than a
decade to her husband, Auguste, and the mother of two children. Both
husband and wife were close to the center of the court of the French
emperor Napoleon. She was a friend of the Empress Josephine. He
was a close adviser to the emperor. Their lives had recently been made
difficult by the divorce of Napoleon and Josephine, which was followed swiftly by the emperor's remarriage. The Rémusats, after a long
time together, were kept apart temporarily while he was in Fontainebleau, at the new court that was growing up around the emperor and
his second wife, Marie-Louise of Austria. Despite this separation, the
divisions between Napoleon and Josephine served to make Claire de

Rémusat more conscious of the harmony between herself and her absent husband.

At present, though, life with the now divorced empress was gloomy. Claire de Rémusat told Auguste in another letter how "all is very sad, as you may suppose. The empress is greatly cast down; she weeps incessantly, and it is really painful to see her." Together with the constant threat of war, this made the times difficult.

She began her current letter by complaining: "I am vexed at the length of your absence." It was as if she was affected by the sadness around her. Yet soon she felt, in contrast, the richness that their relationship had brought to them.

When they first met "in youth," they must have enjoyed the crackle of discovering "a diversity of tastes and opinions." Now that they had been married for years, their relationship had become naturally a more balanced togetherness based upon "harmony and unity." Love changed and developed over time. A stable attachment was also always growing and further deepening. Claire de Rémusat must have been especially aware of the harmony of their present-day situation given the conflict that continued between Josephine and Napoleon. She was not inclined to undervalue their "quieter and safer joys."

A peaceful mood settled over her and she confessed with humor how she was "writing for the pleasure of writing." She did not need the excuse of news to write to her husband. It was an obvious way of being together at a distance. She shared intimate details of the moment: "I am lazily lying in bed; the weather is cold; I have not the least inclination to go out, and find myself very comfortable." She had a little writing desk on her knees, and shared with Auguste "all that comes into my head, or rather my heart." She had shaken off the surrounding gloom.

In that moment of amused self-awareness, as she saw herself writing so freely to her husband, lying at ease in the warmth, she was able to let go of all other concerns and be happy as if they were together— as truly they were.

Life Surpasses Art

Benjamin Haydon, artist,
writing a letter to a friend

WINDSOR, BERKSHIRE · OCTOBER 20, 1819

Here I am, my dear Miss Mitford, sitting by my dearest Mary with all the complacency of a well-behaved husband, writing to you while she is working quietly on some unintelligible part of a lady's costume. The day is beautiful, cool, sunny, and genial, fit for the beauty and gentle looks of such a creature as my wife. You do not know how proud I am of saying: my wife. I never felt half so proud of Solomon *or* Macbeth *[his paintings] as I am of being the husband of this little tender bit of lovely humanity.*

It rained the whole day yesterday; was dark, dingy, dreary and dull out of doors, but within there was a sunbeam gleaming about that made me forget the wind and rain. Mary smiles and says you must not believe one half of what I write now. You must believe all. My understanding never loses its perspicacity, however agitated are my feelings, or tenderly disposed is my heart; therefore you will believe it, I feel sure. People are very curious to see my wife, as everyone seems surprised. "You are a man," wrote a friend, "who I should have thought would have married some young girl at first sight instead of selecting a widow lady." Ha! Ha! I suppose they imagine some old widow, whose face presageth snow instead of rich and rosy youthful beauty. I shall return to town next week and commence my studies. Accept my and my dearest Mary's thanks for your kind congratulations. I hope you will allow me to send you a large bit of wedding cake, and you shall have some to give to every sweet darling you know in your neighborhood, with my best wishes for their happiness.

❧

Benjamin Haydon was an English painter who specialized in grand canvases of classical or biblical stories. After early difficulties, he was now, in his early thirties, a well-regarded artist and had many friends among artists as well as writers, one of whom was his correspondent in this letter, the novelist Mary Russell Mitford.

Haydon was in fact in some difficulty over money. It took a long time to complete his enormous paintings, which the poet Wordsworth declared authentic in "every nostril, every fingernail." As a result, he sold few works and meanwhile his debts were mounting. Nevertheless, in 1819, he married Mary Hyman, a young widow, in defiance of these practical problems.

For a while, life was focused on love, and all he needed for happiness was one great truth: "Here I am." That was enough, being there in the new home with his new bride. All his artistic plans and projects were advancing only slowly toward realization. But love was different—he was "sitting by my dearest Mary." Nothing else was needed. The present moment was all sufficient, being by the side of the woman he loved.

He had an amused sense of himself as "a well-behaved husband," accompanying his wife while she quietly mended her clothes. He did not know what exactly she was doing. He felt as if he had never been allowed into the secret world of a woman before. It was comforting and peaceful there.

The whole day felt right, "beautiful, cool, sunny, and genial." The bright calm suited his mood. His art was all about violence and power; but here, in this moment of domesticity, he recognized a beauty that might be humble but was not therefore inferior to grandeur. He saw how ordinary details added up to a scene of precious value.

His wife joined in the written conversation with his friend as he recorded that "Mary smiles and says you must not believe one half of what I write now." The letter became a playful interchange of love and friendship together.

He began to speculate about people's reactions in his social circle when they would hear of his marriage. They would not realize how gentle and beautiful his Mary was. But this only added to his joy of the secludedness of the moment.

Evening

Moonlight in the Château Garden

Washington Irving, author,
writing in his travel journal

FONTAINEBLEAU, FRANCE · AUGUST 30, 1824

Evening, walk in gardens of the Palace [the royal château]—sociable Englishman hovering about us—our street [in town] a very noisy one—jovial blacksmiths always hammering and singing duets—accompanied by anvil—clanking of sabres—a body of lancers [cavalry soldiers] quartered here—lounging about streets—horses dallying by—arrival and depart of diligences—groups of young lancers about cafés. In other parts of the place a contrast is offered by silent, deserted palaces. Fine effect of moonlight in garden and after leaving the Palace—the moon crescent seen over pinnacles of the Palace mingled with trees of the Queen's garden.

In the garden is a fountain of white stone or marble with bronze stag—beautiful sunset in garden—rosy clouds.

cᑲᗅᑲᕋ

Washington Irving is known around the world as the author of the stories "Rip Van Winkle" and "The Legend of Sleepy Hollow," which were first published in *The Sketch Book of Geoffrey Crayon, Gent.* in 1819/20. He was born in 1783 and grew up in Manhattan, New York, the son of parents who had both emigrated from Britain. Washington Irving left for Europe in 1815, arriving initially in England, where he remained for some years dealing with troubles in the family business, before departing for Germany in 1822. In the summer of 1824 he was visiting Paris. Not far from the French capital was Fontainebleau, a town famous for its royal palace, a great château that had seen kings (as well as the Emperor Napoleon) come and go.

Washington Irving recorded this evening during his weekend stay in Fontainebleau in characteristic clipped phrases that sometimes seem to shuffle the sequence of events. He noted his "walk in gardens of the Palace" and also the amusing detail of an Englishman who was "hovering about us."

199

Then he reported the moment when he came out of his Fontaine-bleau hotel and found the "street a very noisy one." It was not the ordinary bustle of traffic. To his responsive imagination, this place was like the set of a charming opera, full of "jovial blacksmiths" singing their "duets." It had the atmosphere of a stage, like watching a jolly French story complete with orchestral accompaniment. The hammers seemed to be playing the rhythm of a lively song. There were cavalry soldiers hanging about the cafés, swords clanking and horses coming and going. Washington Irving must have enjoyed how stereotypical these scenes outside his hotel were. His breathless phrases are full of pleasure. He was amused and also entranced. He was ready for a special evening experience.

It was all a prelude to the magnificent gardens of Fontainebleau, where he was met by a "fine effect of moonlight" when he came out of the château itself. It was as if the stage lighting had produced a sudden glow of pale silver, now that the music of the streets had fallen silent.

He had a magical moment when the crescent of the moon seemed to rest above the pinnacles and rooftops of the palace and "mingled with" the shadowy outlines of the dark trees.

As the darkness had gathered earlier in the evening, he had seen in the garden a white fountain with the statue of a stag by it, as if enchanted to stillness. The sunset had made the clouds "rosy" and the whole place caught its beauty.

After the singing duets and the rattling swords, the Englishman and the cafés, this château garden brought an equally magical inner peace and happiness to Washington Irving.

A Touch of Autumn

Wang Wei, poet and painter, composing a poem

SOUTH OF XI'AN, CHINA · CA. 759 CE

The vacant hills are fresh with recent rain.
The coming autumn threats in evening's chill.
Amid the firs the moon peeps in again.
Bright flashes o'er the stones each mountain rill.
With chat of maids, who take their homeward way
Their washing done, the bamboo-groves resound.
The fisher's skiff the lotus brushes round:
The water ripples as they stir and sway.
Although the fragrance of the Spring be gone,
Yet Nature's lover well may linger on.

⌒∞⌒

Wang Wei was born around 700 CE in Qi county, in the Chinese province of Shaanxi. When he was in his early twenties, he achieved the rare distinction of being made an "advanced scholar" through the civil service examination. He attained higher office in the provinces but was recalled to the capital, Chang'an (today's Xi'an), in the 730s. His bureaucratic career did not really flourish. Later, in 756, he was captured by rebels during the turmoil of the An Lushan rebellion. Forced to work for them, his life was in danger when the emperor came back to power a few years later. Wang Wei was rescued by the intervention of his brother, a high-ranking administrator. Exhausted by these troubles and saddened by the earlier death of his wife and of his mother, he withdrew to his country retreat south of the capital.

There he wrote many poems about his everyday experiences of the place. He was living in the foothills of the Qinling Mountains, among forests and rivers. He studied Buddhism and developed a style of painting that proved immensely influential. He shared his observations with other poets. This was the heyday of the Tang dynasty but for Wang Wei, these last few years of his life were a time of deep quiet.

This poem describes an experience of the coming of evening at the summer's end. The day had been wet. Now there was the sensation of that rain still lingering in the air as it blew down "fresh" from the hills. Autumn had not yet arrived but he could feel a slight nip of the seasons changing. It was a moment of change, between day and night, light and dark, summer and fall.

He looked at the fir trees and saw the moon through their branches. The moonlight was here and there reflected on the ripples of the rills, the small streams, as they ran down from the mountainsides, bubbling with the recent rainwater. He heard in the distance the "chat of maids," the voices of women going home, finished with their washing by a river. He also heard the soft noise of the boats of the fishermen—perhaps they, too, were finishing their day's work. Behind it all, there was the quiet, persistent sound of water.

The extraordinary peace that Wang Wei felt at that moment, with its evening details of objects and people, shades and sounds, was suffused by absences: rain that was no longer falling, the "vacant hills," and "the fragrance of the Spring be gone."

To start with, his mood might have been a blend of gentle sadness and appreciation for the beauty of the evening. As these different sights and sounds came to him, he mellowed into a moment of contentment, lingering with the last light of the day and a final taste of the summer.

The Music of the Mountain

Hans Christian Andersen, author, writing a letter to a friend

THE BROCKEN, GERMANY · MAY 26, 1831

Here I am sitting on Blocksberg [the Brocken mountain] and writing to you in the middle of a cloud, a nasty cloud which perhaps looks very nice from below, and many a poetical genius wishes himself up in this heavenly land of the mountains; but they should only try it! Here is snow, the fire is lit in the stove, and I have an Englishman for my neighbour. It is quite like winter; I have been obliged to take two glasses of punch, and I am now going to bed, therefore no more of this place.

At this very moment three of the servant girls are dancing outside the window. They have, after the German fashion, flowing cloaks of cotton, and snoods over their heads; they are gathering flowers, while light, misty clouds pass them like lightning; it is like the witch scene in Macbeth! There is a party of thirty besides the other travellers; they have brought musical instruments with them, and play delightfully. As we cannot see anything, I am now going to sleep to sounds of music.

⁓∞⁓

Hans Christian Andersen was in his twenties, only a few years out of school in Copenhagen. He was escaping from an impoverished background with the support of patrons who recognized his literary power. One day he would be the world-famous author of classic fairy tales. Already in 1831 he knew that he was going to be a writer. He had had a first success with a story. But he was not yet sure what kinds of books to write.

In such letters as this one to his friend Mrs. Laessoe back home, he was exploring the possibility of travel writing, which was fashionable at the time. That is why he was staying at this hotel in the Harz Mountains in northern Germany. It must have felt a long way from his native city by the sea: "Here I am sitting on Blocksberg and writing to you in the middle of a cloud, a nasty cloud."

The fire was crackling in the stove. An Englishman was sitting nearby. Though it was almost June, Andersen had two glasses of hot punch to warm up. "It is quite like winter," he remarked. Clearly, to him there was nothing romantic about this evening, and he was ready for bed.

Then, "at this very moment," he stopped complaining. Outside the window he saw three shadowy figures. He noticed their German-style cloaks "and snoods over their heads." It was a strange scene, these young women gathering flowers in the darkness. Forgetting all the discomfort and tedium, he became immersed imaginatively in the moment with those "flowing cloaks of cotton" and the mysterious light. He was no longer cynical. Instead he was bewitched by the appeal of these women. And why were they gathering flowers on this cold and misty evening?

Andersen began to play with different associations. Everybody knew the German folktale of Walpurgis Night—the eve of May Day—when witches were believed to hold their celebrations on the Brocken. And then there was Shakespeare's play *Macbeth*, which he had read when he was eleven. He loved it and he had read it many times since. For him, those three "servant girls" were instantly transformed into the three witches, and the clouds on a German mountain were turned into the fog on a Scottish heath. He had a feeling of magic even though he knew better.

Then the spell was diluted. Soon these "witches" had companions. A crowd was gathering, complete with musical instruments.

Andersen decided to retire to bed after all. As he did, his sense of magic returned. The melody flowed into his chamber and he was "going to sleep to sounds of music." The present moment was suddenly beautiful and complete. He had no lingering thoughts about future prospects as he slipped gently and happily to sleep, accompanied by the music of the mountain.

Books That Bring the Past Alive

Niccolò Machiavelli, politician and philosopher,
writing a letter to a friend

NEAR FLORENCE · DECEMBER 10, 1513

When evening comes, I return home and enter my study; on the threshold
I take off my workday clothes, covered with mud and dirt, and put on the
garments of court and palace. Fitted out appropriately, I step inside the ven-
erable courts of the ancients, where, solicitously received by them, I nourish
myself on that food that alone is mine and for which I was born; where I am
unashamed to converse with them and to question them about the motives
for their actions, and they, out of their human kindness, answer me. And for
four hours at a time, I feel no boredom, I forget all my troubles, I do not dread
poverty, and I am not terrified by death. I absorb myself into them completely.
And because Dante says that no-one understands anything unless he retains
what he has understood, I have jotted down what I have profited from in their
conversation and composed a short study, "About Princes," in which I delve as
deeply as I can into the ideas concerning this topic, discussing the definition of
a princedom, the categories of princedoms, how they are acquired, how they
are retained, and why they are lost. And if ever any whimsy of mine has given
you pleasure, this one should not displease you.

⟨∞⟩

Niccolò Machiavelli was born in 1469. He rose to become a powerful
man in his native city of Florence. By 1511, he had been a diplomat
and minister in the republican government for a number of years.
Then, in 1512, the Spanish army overthrew the republican regime,
leading to the return of the powerful Medici family in Florence.
Machiavelli was accused of conspiracy against them. He was put in
prison and tortured. After some months, he was released and allowed
to go into exile on his father's rural estate at San Casciano, south of
Florence. That is where he wrote this letter to his friend Francesco
Vettori, who was a diplomat living in Rome.

Machiavelli had been used to a grand lifestyle. Now he lived on what
to him felt like a farm, surrounded by fields and trees. He spent his days

rambling and pausing at the local inns. He was not impoverished or in hardship, but he was bored. He had never been interested in country life. While not far away from his beloved city, this was all alien to him.

Yet at the end of each weary day, he had a path that led back to happiness, perhaps even to happiness deeper than any in his days of success and honor. Taking off the ordinary clothes in which he wandered the woods and meadows, he dressed himself as if for the grand life from which he was now exiled. But instead of visiting the courts and palaces of his contemporaries, he stepped into his own study and, by opening the leather-bound books with their texts in Latin, he met the gathered spirits of the past, particularly the spirits of ancient Greece and Rome. Seated in this room, he read historians and philosophers, letters and poems. At last, he was safe from the boredom and anxiety of his present world.

Whereas Machiavelli's contemporaries shunned him—he was too dangerous to be connected with—the classical authors "out of their human kindness, answer me." He had no need any longer to feel ashamed. He was free from the routine of country life and he could temporarily perhaps find relief from the memories of his painful imprisonment. Death itself fell silent. After all, these kind literary friends were centuries old themselves. Immortality beckoned.

It was a deep, rich, and long moment—"for four hours at a time"— during which he turned those pages and in his thoughts conversed with his ancient friends. It was the kind of extended happiness in which the rest of life fades into the background and then disappears altogether: "I absorb myself into them completely." He was entirely himself, doing the things "for which I was born." Yet he was freed of all self-consciousness and self-concern.

Out of the happiness of such evenings, there was born one of the immortal books of world civilization: Machiavelli's *The Prince*. It was not ambition, danger, or suffering that nurtured the inspiration for this work. On the contrary: the ideas flowed out of these happy hours, being at ease, in his study. No doubt the experiences of his political and public past were a part of the achievement. Certainly, the book itself is full of worldly wisdom and experience. Yet its origins lay elsewhere, in the to and fro of the perfect imaginary conversations in the study of a countryside home outside Florence as the evening settled over the woodland.

A Sense of Beauty as the Sun Sets

Unknown Author, composing a poem

NEAR OSAKA, JAPAN · BEFORE CA. 759 CE

I pass the sparkling sea of Naniwa
And by the sun's going down I am beyond Mt. Kusaka where the grass
*   is yielding under foot.*
You who are no less pretty than the blossoming flowers that crowd
*   the mountain—*
Before you know it I will be back to see you.

⟶∞⟵

This description of a good feeling in the evening comes from the oldest Japanese anthology of poems, called *Manyoshu* (*Collection of Ten Thousand Leaves*). The volume was completed around 759 CE at the imperial court in Kyoto by leading scholars. The large majority of the 4,500 poems of different periods were by aristocratic and court authors. This poem, though, was different. It was included anonymously, with the explanation that the writer was of too humble a rank to be named in this noble company. Now it gives us a snatch of daily happiness from the world beyond the court.

The Nara period in Japan, during much of the eighth century CE, was widely influenced by Chinese ideas; and indeed, the script in the *Manyoshu* used Chinese characters to express Japanese sentences. The delicate sense of the everyday moment has strong links with Tang Chinese culture. But there is also a distinctive and very personal feeling to the evening moment here.

The author begins his poem by the sea. The waves are shining in the sun at Naniwa (present-day Osaka). Then he records a journey inland as the daylight begins to fade and the night comes closer. The time in this snapshot from a man's life long ago changes simply with the natural light, not due to any clock. His was not social time but natural time, the rhythm of the sun in the sky. When he began, the sea was sparkling. His journey then took him beyond a grassy mountainside as the sun sank lower in the skies.

This was a man for whom life must have been very present in the passing minutes of that evening. The background of his life is lost to us, since he probably never tried to record it. But those sensations as he looked at the sea and the sunset were preserved in that ancient *Collection of Ten Thousand Leaves*. There is something strange and touching about how these passionate instants of the joy of life on a Japanese evening survived so many centuries.

His consciousness is preserved in the sights and sounds as he left behind those sparkling waves and crossed the grassy land. There, on all sides of the mountain, were "blossoming flowers." They were probably shrubs known as *ashibi*, an intense swirl of color flowing over the land.

He must have felt a kind of all-embracing sensation of beauty. He found himself addressing his thoughts to the woman he loved. Her beauty, too, was here around him now, present to his eyes like the natural world in the evening light. Her presence was part of these blossoming riches, the flowers "that crowd the mountain."

Darkness was falling. His mind flashed ahead now, to the finish of this journey. Soon he would be with her. The meeting, the embrace of love, they would be the final expression of this evening when his world was beautiful.

The Heart Comes Home to Quietness

Dorothy Wordsworth, writer,
recording the day in her diary

GRASMERE, CUMBRIA · MAY 16, 1800

Warm and mild, after a fine night of rain [. . .] I carried a basket for mosses, and gathered some wild plants. Oh! that we had a book of botany. All flowers now are gay and deliciously sweet. The primrose still prominent; the later flowers and the shiny foxgloves very tall, with their heads budding. I went forward round the lake at the foot of Loughrigg Fell. I was much amused with the busyness of a pair of stonechats [birds]; their restless voices as they skimmed along the water, following each other, their shadows under them, and their returning back to the stones on the shore, chirping with the same unwearied voice. Could not cross the water, so I went round by the stepping-stones [. . .] Rydale [lake] was very beautiful, with spear-shaped streaks of polished steel. Grasmere [lake] very solemn in the last glimpse of twilight. It calls home the heart to quietness.

⟨∞⟩

Dorothy Wordsworth had come to live in the village of Grasmere in the mountainous English Lake District. She was keeping house for her brother William, already a well-known poet. They had grown up not far away but had recently been living in the southwest of England. She was twenty-eight in the late spring of 1800.

She kept a private journal that made her posthumously famous in her own right. On this day she went for a ramble alone, which ended in a special moment by the two nearby lakes, "Rydale" (Rydal Water) and Grasmere.

Her words offer a string of little pleasures. The air was soft and fresh: "Warm and mild, after a fine night of rain." In the woods, by the lake beyond the village, some of the plants were strange to her but she wanted desperately to know what they were: "Oh! that we had a book of botany." But she was able to set aside these concerns and simply enjoy the sight of "flowers [. . .] gay and deliciously sweet." Her senses responded to the immediate appeal of the late spring scene.

She walked along the lakeside, underneath the slope of Lough-rigg Fell, a steep hill. There she was entertained by two birds as they "skimmed along the water." Her eyes followed the flight of the stone-chats, "their shadows under them." Every detail stood out for her, even these small spots of darkness sliding over the water's edge.

The afternoon was slowly turning into evening. Dorothy Words-worth wanted to set off home, which meant crossing the little river that flowed between the two lakes. She found she had no path to "cross the water" until she "went round by the stepping-stones."

As she balanced her way from stone to stone in the little river, the sun had almost set and the last light gleamed in the sky.

On one side was Rydal Water, "very beautiful, with spear-shaped streaks of polished steel," where the silver gleam of the evening was reflected. In the other direction was Grasmere lake, "very solemn in the last glimpse of twilight," still under the darkening sky. It was almost a spiritual experience, though firmly rooted in the sensations of a day's end in this world.

Dorothy Wordsworth had seen many enjoyable things on her day's excursion. Now this evening brought her a moment of deep tranquil-lity: "It calls home the heart to quietness." She also noted that she "had been very melancholy" as she made her way back home, disap-pointed also to have found no letters waiting for her when she called at the village of Clappersgate where they would have been kept for her. She was even tearful, perhaps with some fatigue. Yet at the very conclusion, the joy and peace of the day flowed into her feelings, and "when I came to Grasmere [village] I felt that it did me good." Even the touch of sadness was now part of the profound acceptance and affirmation of life that this evening had given her.

A Stroll along the Water

Henri Frédéric Amiel, philosopher,
writing in his journal

GENEVA · JUNE 16, 1851

This evening I walked up and down on the Pont des Bergues [a bridge in the heart of Geneva], under a clear moonless heaven, delighting in the freshness of the water, streaked with light from the two quays, and glimmering under the twinkling stars. Meeting all these different groups of young people, families, couples, and children, who were returning to their homes, to their garrets or their drawing-rooms, singing or talking as they went, I felt a movement of sympathy for all these passersby; my eyes and ears became those of a poet or a painter; while even one's mere kindly curiosity seems to bring with it a joy in living and in seeing others live.

⌒∞∽

Henri Frédéric Amiel lived in Geneva, in the French-speaking part of Switzerland. He was twenty-nine and had been appointed as professor of aesthetics and French literature at the Academy of Geneva two years earlier. (In 1854, he became a professor of moral philosophy.) He was a private man who enjoyed reading, listening to music, and the beauty of the natural world. He enjoyed conversation, too, and was kind and relaxed with children, though he was not always at ease teaching his students.

He lived alone, and his social life was further constrained by political conflicts that were rife in Geneva at the time. Amiel had become a professor after Geneva's Radical Party had taken over power from the conservative and aristocratic faction. Though Amiel himself was hardly aware of the political issues, his appointment, and others like it, were controversial (because previous professors had left their posts when the regime changed), and this limited his access to the largely aristocratic cultural and intellectual life of the city. He was very much on his own.

On this early summer evening, he felt better. He "walked up and down on the Pont des Bergues," a bridge over the River Rhône where it emerges from Lake Geneva. It was pleasing to be close to "the freshness of the water." Light shone out from the quays onto the dark water. Above, the stars were pinpoints in a clear sky, "twinkling" in the "moonless heaven."

The old city seemed at home with the natural world. Everyone, apparently, had come out for the June night. All kinds of people were walking by the lake. They shared an appreciation of this freshness and the panorama of sky, stars, and water—and the mountains as backdrop.

Amiel noticed the different people: young and old, families and couples, strolling together. And what contrasts between their lives! It was getting later and they were on the way home, but to such varied homes: garrets here, drawing rooms there.

It was their voices that struck him. Perhaps it was getting too dark now to see the faces clearly, but he could hear them all, "singing or talking as they went," filled with an appreciation for life.

The evening brought them all together. Suddenly, Amiel had a sensation almost out of nowhere. He felt connected to his fellow Genevese, and he shared their lives for a moment. They were just "passersby," strangers on a pleasant night: yet at this moment, he "felt a movement of sympathy" for all these individuals walking by the river and the lakeside. They were no longer indifferent, though in a way they were still strangers. He felt as if he were able to embrace them all equally.

He understood something, almost against the grain of his usual thoughts. He realized that to relish his own life, he had to enjoy the presence of other people with their very different and separate lives. Other people made him happy. He discovered in that moment by the evening lake that he felt "a joy in living and in seeing others live."

Amiel's senses were alert and he experienced the scene like "a poet or a painter." People and their activities were sharply real to him. He was used to feeling "kindly curiosity," but now as everyone felt suddenly so real and their lives as deep as his own, this natural interest brimmed over into excited pleasure.

This was perhaps just a passing moment, and it had in a way begun so casually, but it was as deep as any other in a philosopher's thoughtful lifetime.

Sweet Calm after a Storm

Francis Higginson, clergyman and emigrant,
writing in his voyage journal

OFF CAPE ANN, MASSACHUSETTS · JUNE 27, 1629

Saturday a foggy morning; but after eight o'clock in the morning very clear. The wind being somewhat contrary at south and by west, we tacked to and again with getting little [change], but with much ado. About four o'clock in the afternoon, having with much pain compassed the harbour, and being ready to enter the same (see how things may suddenly change!), there came a fearful gust of wind and rain and thunder and lightning, whereby we were borne with no little terror and trouble to our mariners, having very much ado to loose down the sails when the fury of the storm struck us. But, God be praised, it lasted but a while, and soon abated again. And hereby the Lord showed us what he could have done with us, if it had pleased him. But, blessed be God, he soon removed this storm, and it was a fair and sweet evening.

We had a westerly wind, which brought us, between five and six o'clock, to a fine and sweet harbour, seven miles from the head point of Cape Ann.

༺∞༻

Francis Higginson was born around 1587, in Leicestershire, central England. He was the son of a vicar, and when he graduated from Cambridge University in 1610 he was set to follow in his father's footsteps. He did become a Church of England minister, also near Leicester, but by 1627 he had joined the Puritan movement, in conflict with the bishops. In 1628 the archbishop of Canterbury began a concerted attempt to impose discipline on those members of the Church of England who sympathized with nonconformism. Fearing imprisonment, Francis Higginson agreed to join a party of emigrants organized by the Massachusetts Bay Company. On April 25, 1629, he and his wife, Ann, with their children, left from Gravesend on board the *Talbot*, bound for Massachusetts.

On Saturday, June 27, their ordeal at sea was nearly over. They were approaching the Massachusetts coast at Cape Ann. The "foggy morning" seems to have turned into a fine day. But suddenly, "about four o'clock in the afternoon," the sea became rough with "a fearful gust of wind and rain and thunder and lightning." Such a storm was bound to impress a devout man of the time as a divine warning. But there was also the drama of events in front of his eyes, the sailors fighting to keep the ship seaworthy and the fear that at this final moment, so close to the harbor, all their sufferings on the way across the Atlantic would be in vain.

The raging wind and driving rain were intense but fortunately did not last too long. The afternoon had gone with the storm and there was a moment, after the skies had calmed, when Francis Higginson felt the simple joy of "a fair and sweet evening." Now he had the great pleasure of just being alive, as that afternoon of "terror" ended in calm. For Higginson, further trials lay ahead and he would die just over a year later, after playing a short but leading role in the life of the new settlement of Salem. Yet this moment speaks for itself.

After the storm had passed, the benign aura of this place seemed to embrace the emigrants once again, as it had the previous day when their approach to the New World was welcomed, so it felt, by beautiful yellow flowers on the very surface of the sea: "The sea was abundantly stored with rockweed and yellow flowers, like gilliflowers [. . .] The nearer we came to the shore, the more flowers in abundance, sometimes scattered abroad, sometimes joined in sheets nine or ten yards long, which we supposed to be brought from the low meadows by the tide. Now what with fine woods and green trees by land, and these yellow flowers painting the sea, made all desirous to see our new paradise of New England, whence we saw such forerunning signals of fertility afar off."

Those beautiful waters had darkened for a little while but now, in the mellowed light of evening, the sense of fulfillment and hope returned. Each of those two days had its moments of happiness, which this day's ending brought to completion.

A Divine Little Book

George Ridpath, historian and vicar, writing in his diary

STICHILL, SCOTTISH BORDERS · DECEMBER 13, 1755

Prepared for tomorrow. Read some of the History of the British Empire in America, *vol. 1, which I got today from the library. Read* Letters to Atticus *[by Cicero] in the evening. And slept on Epictetus, a divine little work which I had grown pretty much unacquainted with.*

⁕

George Ridpath was born in about 1717, the eldest son of a Scottish church minister. He was educated at Edinburgh University and ordained in the Church of Scotland. In 1742, he became vicar of the village of Stichill, near the border town of Kelso in Scotland, and remained there until his death in 1772. He married Wilhelmina Dawson in 1764 and they had one daughter—but at the time he wrote this entry in his diary, he was still a single man and his manse was shared with his widowed mother. He was a scholar but not a deeply religious man. His reading was in history and philosophy and he tended to write his Sunday sermons only on Saturday, as he mentioned here: "Prepared for tomorrow."

This December Saturday had plenty of reading in it. The vicar was busy with John Oldmixon's *History of the British Empire in America*, published in 1708. (He had obtained a copy of the book in Kelso.) This was partly his interest as an author, since he wrote local history himself. (His *Border History of England and Scotland* was published posthumously in 1776 by his brother Philip, also a minister.) Next he turned to the writings of the great Roman author Cicero, whose *Letters to Atticus* were the model for polite correspondence and reflective conversation.

But as the evening was coming to an end and he was ready for sleep, George Ridpath picked a book by Epictetus (who died around 135 CE), a philosophical writer and freed slave who was born in what is now Turkey, lived in Rome and then in Greece. His main work, *The Discourses*, which would have been Ridpath's nightcap book, was a witty and epigrammatic defense of Epicurean philosophy, one of whose central principles was the focus on living a modestly contented life in this world. It is about how to live, the restraint of emotion and the attainment of balanced peace. Epictetus also argued for the tolerant acceptance of different religions. It seems to have been exactly what Ridpath enjoyed after composing his Sunday sermon.

He sometimes recorded the particular book he read last at night with a lovely expressive gratitude, saying as with Epictetus that he "slept on" the work. These books he curled up with last thing before blowing out the candles were texts he particularly liked, including also the poetry of the Roman author Horace. He must have had a particularly fine read of Epictetus this evening.

This enjoyment came as a bit of a surprise. He had "grown pretty much unacquainted" with the *Discourses* and so the short book felt again as if it was a new discovery. He loved reading this "divine little work": here "little" and "divine" balance each other beautifully to make a touching acknowledgment that the ancient philosopher's thought was inspiring and also on a human scale, profound yet not overwhelming. The vicar's use of "divine" here is also amusing since it was not a religious book.

Two days later, on Monday the 15th, he spent some time working on a biblical commentary, but it was once again his evening read that drew an expression of appreciative pleasure: "At night read Epictetus with vast relish." For George Ridpath, it was a real treat to settle down with a good book on a wintry evening, his sermon done for another week, his thought free to wander as he drifted toward sleep. It was the perfect end to the day and also the best of ways to welcome the night.

At Ease Watching the Boats

Walt Whitman, poet,
writing in his diary

SARNIA, ONTARIO · JUNE 19, 1880

Sunset on the St. Clair. I am writing this on Front Street, close by the river—the St. Clair—on a bank. The setting sun, a great blood-red ball, is just descending on the Michigan shore, throwing a bright crimson track across the water to where I stand. The river is full of row-boats and shells, with their crews of young fellows, or single ones, out practising—a handsome, inspiriting sight [. . .]

As I write, a long shell, with its crew of four stript to their rowing shirts, sweeps swiftly past, the oars rattling in their row-locks.

Opposite, a little south, on the Michigan shore, stretches Port Huron. It is a still, moist, voluptuous evening, the twilight deepening apace. In the vapors fly bats and myriads of big insects. A solitary robin is whistling his call, followed by mellow clucks, in some trees near. The panting of the locomotive and measured roll of cars comes from over shore, and occasionally an abrupt snort or screech, diffused in space. With all these utilitarian episodes, it is a lovely, soft, voluptuous scene, a wondrous half-hour for sunset, and then the long rose-tinged half-light with a touch of gray we sometimes have stretched out in June at day-close. How musical the cries and voices floating in from the river! Mostly while I have been here I have noticed those handsome shells and oar-boats, some of them rowing superbly.

❧

Walt Whitman had just turned sixty-one in June of 1880. He had published the first of several editions of his great lifetime collection of poems, *Leaves of Grass*, back in 1855. He was widely respected as a poet by critics and readers. But he was also short of money and in very poor health, having suffered a stroke.

Whitman had come to Canada for several weeks at the invitation of a younger man, the psychiatrist Richard Bucke, who admired his work. He began his visit with Bucke and his wife at their home in London, Ontario. From there Whitman took a train to Sarnia on the St. Clair River (where Richard Bucke had previously worked and lived) and stayed there for a few days. He could see Port Huron, Michigan, on the opposite shore.

On this June evening, he was at ease. He had always loved looking out over water and watching people on their journeys. His great poem "Crossing Brooklyn Ferry" had expressed his passion for the maritime life of his native New York. But he could appreciate this place, too, in its different way.

He gazed across the St. Clair at the different rowing boats. The rowers went past with ease and strength. He admired such flexibility and power but now it also carried the slight sadness of the contrast with his own age and lack of youthful athleticism. He turned his gaze overhead, a connoisseur of skies. Compared to New York and New Jersey, where he now lived, this was rather another world. He had become the voice of urban energy. Yet here, he was happy to find a gentler rhythm.

Walt Whitman's moment of happiness here was made up of contraries: the whistling of the robin and the locomotive sound; the machines and the rowing boats; the approaching night and the last glimmering of daylight. On this evening, the opposites were reconciled: past and future, land and water, urban and rural life, youth and age. Under it all there ran a deeper resolution, between Whitman's strong self and the world beyond him, which would outlast even his immense personality. Everything was at peace in this gentle moment, as tensions had slipped away.

A Poet's Son Goes to Bed

Ann Yearsley, poet and author,
composing a personal preface to a poem

BRISTOL · FEBRUARY 27, 1795

Begun from the circumstance of the moment, and prolonged as the images of
memory arose in the mind of the author, February 27, 1795.
    Author (to her son): Go you to bed, my boy.
    Son: Do you write tonight?
    Author: I do.
    Son (laying his watch on the table): See, how late!
    Author: No matter—You can sleep.
    How patiently toils on this little watch!
    My veins beat to its motion.

⚬◊⚬

Ann Yearsley had seven children. This February evening, when she
was in her early forties, she was sitting by the bedside of one of her
sons.

    She had had an unusual life. Her parents were poor, her mother
being a milkwoman. Some poems Ann Yearsley had written came to
the attention of a lady (herself a noted author) who recognized her
talent. Yearsley published her first collection of poetry in 1785 and it
was immediately well-received. Among her subsequent works was
the "Poem on the Inhumanity of the Slave Trade."

    The money from her authorship had improved life for Ann Years-
ley and her husband, who was a yeoman farmer. But a quarrel with
her patroness had ended that peaceful time. Still, she had also published a novel, and a play of hers had been performed in Bath.

    As she was sitting with her son, she recorded this precious moment.
She began with the date: February 27, 1795. She remembered the
snatch of conversation with him, an ordinary domestic exchange at
the end of the day. "'Go you to bed, my boy.'" It was what any par-
ent would say; it has been said countless times down the centuries on
quiet evenings. He was not quite sleepy yet. Her energy was what

had kept him awake. He knew she was not going to sleep, and he wished to share the evening: "'Do you write tonight?'" Her writing ran through his young life.

"'I do.'" She was calm and reassuring, purposeful and at ease. He pointed to his pocket watch, a proud possession: "'See, how late!'" Perhaps he wanted her not to write tonight, to be with him instead. She soothed him: "'No matter—You can sleep.'" There was nothing special about this hour of the day, nothing to worry the child. He went to sleep.

She heard the ticking of the watch, like the beating of her son's heart or the sound of his breathing. In the next minutes, she composed a beginning for her poem: "How patiently toils on this little watch!" Like herself, even and unstoppable. "My veins beat to its motion." She began to write, a long poem full of ideas and arguments.

This was a moment of simple truth, peace at the end of the day. That is why she recorded it, before she commenced to write the poem. In that moment, life was integrated and in balance. Both mother and poet, she sat happily by her child's bedside.

It was a moment of quiet joy attained against great pressure. When the noted author Horace Walpole had agreed to sponsor Ann Yearsley's poems initially, he expressed a concern that such support might distract her from her duties to her family: "Were I not persuaded by the samples you have sent me, madam, that this woman has talents, I should not advise her encouraging her propensity, lest it should divert her from the care of her family." She had overcome these prejudices and earned this moment of complete happiness.

Notes

MORNING

A Sunday Ride without Worry • Isabella Bird
Isabella Bird, *A Lady's Life in the Rocky Mountains* (London, John Murray) 1879

Jackdaw Song Breaks the Mist • John James Audubon
John James Audubon, *Audubon and His Journals, Vol. 1, European Journal,* edited by Maria Rebecca Audubon and Elliott Coues (New York, C. Scribner's Sons) 1897

A Plunge into Cold Water • Friedrich Schleiermacher
Friedrich Schleiermacher, *The Life of Schleiermacher, as Unfolded in his Autobiography and Letters,* translated by F. Rowan (London, Smith Elder) 1860

The First Glow of Sun on the Wet Mountain • Hsu Hsia-k'o
Hsu Hsia-k'o, *Travel Diaries of Hsu Hsia-k'o,* translated by Li Chi (Hong Kong, The Chinese University of Hong Kong) 1974

Keen Air on Christmas Day • Henry White
Henry White, *Henry White: Notes on the Parishes of Fyfield, Kimpton, Penton Mewsey, Weyhill and Wherwell, in the County of Hampshire,* revised and edited by Edward Doran Webb (Salisbury, Bennett Brothers) 1898

A Glorious Sunrise Dispels the Gloom • Patrick Kenny
Patrick Kenny, "Diary of Rev. Patrick Kenny," *Records of the American Catholic Historical Society of Philadelphia* 1898 p. 249ff

The Urge to Linger in a Warm Bed • Marcus Aurelius
Marcus Aurelius, *Meditations,* translated by Richard Graves (London, Robinson) 1792

Winter Dawn in the Cathedral Close • Anna Seward
Anna Seward, "Sonnet XL. December Morning" from *The Poetical Works* (Edinburgh, Ballantyne and Co) 1810

FRIENDSHIP

Time Together with an Ancient Book • Willem de Clercq
Dagboek van Willem de Clerq 1811–1830. Passage translated from the
original French by George Myerson
Original French at http://www.inghist.nl/retroboeken/declercq/

A Climb to the Top of the Hill • Kamo no Chomei
Passage translated from the original Japanese by Alex Dudoq de Wit
An edition of the whole text: Kamo no Chomei, *Ho-jo-ki*, translated by
F. Victor Dickins (London, Gowans and Grey) 1907

A Breakfast Served with Stories and Laughter • George Cutler
Emily Vanderpoel, *Chronicles of a Pioneer School from 1792 to 1833* (Cambridge, Mass., Harvard University Press) 1903

The Freedom of Dancing through the Night • Robert Burns
Robert Burns, *The Works of Robert Burns*, edited by James Currie (London, Cadell and Davies) 1806

In Anticipation of a Gentleman's Visit • Mary Russell Mitford
Mary Russell Mitford, *The Life of Mary Russell Mitford Related in a Selection from Her Letters to Her Friends*, edited by Alfred L'Estrange (London, R. Bentley) 1870

The Familiar Delight of Chitchat • Sarah Connell
Sarah Connell Ayer, *Diary of Sarah Connell Ayer* (Andover and Newburyport, Lefavor-Tower Company) 1910

A Casual Dinner Party • Horace
Horace, *Odes, Satires and Epistles*, translated by Thomas Creech (London, Tonson) 1730

A Free Piano Concert • Robert Schumann
Robert Schumann, *Early Letters of Robert Schumann*, translated by May Herbert (London, George Bell and Sons) 1888

GARDEN

A Glad Return to the Old Pine Tree • Tao Yuanming
Selection of Tao Yuanming's work in *Gems of Chinese Literature*, translated and edited by Herbert A. Giles (Shanghai, Kelly and Walsh) 1922

A Touch of Spring • Thomas Gray
Thomas Gray, "Gardening," January 1755–March 1756, in *Gentleman's Magazine*, 24 September 1845

Floral Abundance • Mary Dawson-Damer
Mary Damer, *Diary of a Tour in Greece, Turkey, Egypt, and the Holy Land* (London, H. Colburn) 1841

The Hours before Dawn at the Imperial Court • Murasaki Shikibu
Passage translated from the original Japanese by Alex Dudoq de Wit
An edition of the whole text: Murasaki Shikibu, *The Diary of Murasaki Shikibu*, in *Diaries of Court Ladies of Old Japan*, translated by Annie Shepley Omori and Kochi Doi (Boston and New York, Houghton Mifflin Company) 1920

Perfect Fragrance • Ogier Ghiselin de Busbecq
Ogier Ghiselin de Busbecq, *The Life and Letters of Ogier Ghiselin de Busbecq*, translated and edited by Charles Thornton Forster and F. H. Blackburn Daniell (London, C. K. Paul) 1881

The Pleasant Distraction of a Blooming Greenhouse • William Cowper
William Cowper, "A Letter to Unwin, June 8, 1783" from *The Unpublished and Uncollected Poems*, edited by T. Wright (London, T. F. Unwin) 1900

The Manmade Rainbow • Michel de Montaigne
Michel de Montaigne, *The Journal of Montaigne's Travels in Italy by Way of Switzerland and Germany in 1580 and 1581*, translated and edited by W. G. Waters (London, John Murray) 1903

Flowers and Fruits Blaze for a Birthday • Oliver Wendell Holmes
Oliver Wendell Holmes, *Life and Letters of Oliver Wendell Holmes*, edited by John Torrey Morse (Boston and New York, Houghton, Mifflin and Co.) 1896

FAMILY

The Sweet Thought of the Children • Yamanoue no Okura
Passage translated from the original Japanese by Alex Dudoq de Wit
Selection of the work available in *The Sacred Books and Early Literature of the East with an Historical Survey and Descriptions, Vol. 13*, edited by Charles F. Horne (New York, Parke, Austin, and Lipscomb) 1917

An Outing to the Park • Charlotte Bousfield
Charlotte Bousfield, *The Bousfield Diaries*, edited by Richard Smart (Bedfordshire Historical Record Society/Boydell Press) 2007

Pride in an Unfinished New Home • Tryphena White
Tryphena Ely White, *Tryphena Ely White's Journal; Being a Record, Written One Hundred Years Ago, of the Daily Life of a Young Lady of Puritan Heritage* (New York, The Grafton Press) 1904

Together Again, At Last • Du Fu
Du Fu, in *Gems of Chinese Verse*, translated and edited by W. J. B. Fletcher (Shanghai, Commercial Press) 1919

Deep Gratitude for Health • John Hull
John Hull, "Notebook," edited by Thomas Lechford in *Archæologia Americana. Transactions and Collections, Vol. 3* (Worcester, American Antiquarian Society) 1857

A Father's Gift of Fruit and Sugar • Edmund Verney
Lady Frances Parthenope Verney and Lady Margaret Maria Williams-Hay Verney, *Memoirs of the Verney Family, Vol. 4* (London and New York, Longmans, Green & Co.) 1892

The Loving Presence of Her Children • Hannah Mary Rathbone
Deborah Reynolds, *The Reynolds-Rathbone Diaries and Letters 1793–1839*, edited by Mrs. Eustace Greg (Printed for Private Circulation) 1905

A Warm Welcome by the In-Laws • Ann Warder
Ann Warder, "Extracts from the Diary of Mrs. Ann Warder," in *The Pennsylvania Magazine of History and Biography* 1893

LEISURE

The Amazing Pelican • John Evelyn
John Evelyn, *Diary and Correspondence, Vol. 1* (London, Bell and Daldy) 1870

The Count's Invitation to a Ball • Mary Wortley Montagu
Mary Wortley Montagu, *Letters of Lady Mary Wortley Montagu: Written during Her Travels in Europe, Asia and Africa to Persons of Distinction, Men of Letters, &c. in Different Parts of Europe* (London, Cassell and Murray) 1779

The Governor's Guests • Ouyang Xiu
Ouyang Xiu, in *Gems of Chinese Literature*, translated and edited by Herbert A. Giles (Shanghai, Kelly and Walsh) 1922

On Top of an Active Volcano • Mary Berry
Mary Berry, *Extracts of the Journals and Correspondence of Miss Berry: From the Year 1783 to 1852*, edited by Lady Theresa Lewis (London, Longmans Green) 1865

A Visit to a Literary Salon • Karl August Varnhagen von Ense
Kate Vaughan Jennings, *Rahel: Her Life and Letters* (London, H. S. King) 1876

· *Notes* ·

A Doorway into Antiquity • Benjamin Silliman
   Benjamin Silliman, *A Journal of Travels in England, Holland, and Scotland, and of Two Passages over the Atlantic, in the Years 1805 and 1806* (Boston, printed by T. B. Wait and Co. for Howe and Deforest, and Increase Cook and Co. Newhaven) 1812

The Landscape Painting • Emma Willard
   Emma Willard, *Journal and Letters, from France and Great-Britain* (Troy, N. Tuttle) 1833

Magic Lights and Fireworks under the Moon • Jane Knox
   Memoirs of a Vanished Generation 1813–1855, edited by Warenne Blake (London and New York, J. Lane) 1909

NATURE

The Bliss of Skating • George Head
   George Head, *Forest Scenes and Incidents, in the Wilds of North America: Being a Diary of a Winter's Route from Halifax to the Canadas* (London, John Murray) 1838

An Amusing Owl • Gilbert White
   Gilbert White, *The Natural History and Antiquities of Selborne* (London, Longman and Co.) 1837

A Vast Sheet of Frozen Water • William Whewell
   Janet Douglas, *The Life and Selections from the Correspondence of William Whewell* (London, C. K. Paul) 1881

The First Sight of the Mountains • Lucy Larcom
   Daniel Dulany Addison, *Lucy Larcom: Life, Letters and Diary* (Boston and New York, Houghton, Mifflin and Co.) 1894

The Celebrated Pine Tree • Matsuo Basho
   Passage translated from the original Japanese by Alex Dudoq de Wit
   An edition of the whole text: Matsuo Basho, *Back Roads to Far Towns*, translated by Cid Corman and Kamaike Susumu (Buffalo, White Pine Press) 2004

The Wonderful Mist of the Waterfall • John Goldie
   John Goldie, *Diary of a Journey through Upper Canada and Some of the New England States*, 1819 (Toronto, W. Tyrell) 1897

New Year's Day in the Heavens and on Earth • Hattori Ransetsu
   Haiku translated from the original Japanese by Alex Dudoq de Wit
   Selected haikus by Ransetsu, including an earlier version of this poem,

225

found in *The Sacred Books and Early Literature of the East with an Histori-cal Survey and Descriptions, Vol. 13*, edited by Charles F. Horne (New York, Parke, Austin, and Lipscomb) 1917

On Top of the World • Edward Price
Edward Price, *Norway and Its Scenery, Comprising the Journal of a Tour by Edward Price, Esq. with Considerable Additions*, edited and compiled by Thomas Forester (London, Henry G. Bohn) 1853

A Fine White Beach • Hannah Callender
George Vaux, "Extracts from the Diary of Hannah Callender," in *The Pennsylvania Magazine of History and Biography* 1888

The Source of the River • William Turner
William Turner, *Journal of a Tour in the Levant* (London, John Murray) 1820

FOOD AND DRINK

The Peerless Plum • Ibn Battuta
Sir Henry Yule, Odorico (da Pordenone), Rashid al-Din Habib, Francesco Balducci Pegolotti, Joannes de Marignolis, Ibn Batuta, and Bento de Góis, *Cathay and the Way Thither: Being a Collection of Medieval Notices of China, Vol. 2* (Printed for the Hakluyt Society) 1866

Home-Style Cooking on the Wagon Trail • Lodisa Frizzell
Lodisa Frizzell, *Across the Plains to California in 1852*, edited by Victor Hugo Paltsits (New York, The New York Public Library) 1915

A Philosopher's Last Taste of Life • Hermippus
Diogenes Laertes, *The Lives of the Philosophers*, translated by C. D. Yonge (London, Henry Bohn) 1853

The Sea Air Gives a Good Appetite • Thomas Turner
Thomas Turner, "Extracts from the Diary of Thomas Turner," *Sussex Archeological Collections* XI 1859

A Handful of Refreshing Well Water • Lady Sarashina
Passage translated from the original Japanese by Alex Dudoq de Wit
An edition of the whole text: Lady Sarashina, *The Sarashina Diary*, in *Diaries of Court Ladies of Old Japan*, translated by Annie Shepley Omori and Kochi Doi (Boston and New York, Houghton Mifflin Company) 1920

A Tasty Dinner in a Rustic Tavern • Cyrus P. Bradley
Cyrus P. Bradley, "Diary 1818–1838," *Ohio Archaeological and Historical Society Quarterly* 1906

The Excellence of Marinaded Pilchards • Humphry Davy
T. E. Thorpe, *Humphrey Davy: Poet and Philosopher* (London, Cassell)
1896

A Great Plenty of Party Treats • Anna Winslow
Anna Green Winslow, *Diary of Anna Green Winslow, a Boston Schoolgirl of
1771*, edited by Alice Morse Earle (Boston and New York, Houghton,
Mifflin and Co.) 1894

WELL-BEING

A Landscape Fit for a Stroll • Thomas Green
Thomas Green, *Extracts from the Diary of a Lover of Literature* (Ipswich,
John Raw) 1810

The Joy of Coming Home • Seydi Ali Reis
Seydi Ali Reis, in *The Sacred Books and Early Literature of the East, Vol.
6: Medieval Arabic, Moorish and Turkish*, edited by Charles F. Horne (New
York, Parke, Austin, and Lipscomb) 1917

A World in Bloom • Pehr Kalm
Peter Kalm, *Travels into North America*, translated by Johann Reinhold
Forster (London, Eyres) 1771

Home, Sweet Home • Jane Welsh Carlyle
Jane Welsh Carlyle, *Letters and Memorials of Jane Welsh Carlyle*, edited by
James Anthony Froude (New York, Harper) 1883

A Traveler's Sweeping Prospect • Benjamin of Tudela
Benjamin of Tudela, in *The Sacred Books and Early Literature of the East,
Vol. 4: Medieval Hebrew: The Midrash; The Kabbalah*, edited by Charles F.
Horne (New York, Parke, Austin, and Lipscomb) 1917

The Joy of Finding a Vocation • Jarena Lee
Jarena Lee, *Religious Experience and Journal of Mrs. Jarena Lee, Giving
an Account of Her Call to Preach the Gospel, Revised and Corrected from the
Original Manuscript Written by Herself* (published for the author in Philadelphia) 1849

Winter Sunshine on a Warm Wall • George Eliot
George Eliot, *George Eliot's Life as Related in Her Letters and Journals*,
edited by J. W. Cross (New York, Harper) 1885

A Peaceful, Late-Night Bath • Walter Scott
Walter Scott, *The Journal of Sir Walter Scott* (New York, Burt Franklin) 1890

A Long and Rewarding Life • Ptah-Hotep
Hardwicke D. Rawnsley, *Notes for the Nile: Together with a Metrical Rendering of the Hymns of Ancient Egypt and of the Precepts of Ptah-Hotep* (New York, Putnam) 1892

A Cottage Near the Sea • William Blake
William Blake, *The Letters of William Blake*, edited by Archibald Russell (London, Methuen) 1906

CREATIVITY

A Shady Grove on a Hot Day • Sappho
H. T. Wharton, *Sappho: Memoir, Text, Selected Renderings* (London, John Lane) 1895

The Pleasure of Mathematical Solutions • Bhaskara
Henry Thomas Colebrooke, *Algebra, with Arithmetic and Mensuration, from the Sanskrit of Brahmegupta and Bhascara* (London, John Murray) 1817

A Day among Great Thinkers • Ralph Thoresby
Ralph Thoresby, *The Diary of Ralph Thoresby (1677–1724)* (London, H. Colburn and R. Bentley) 1830

A Long-Sought Great Idea • Anselm of Canterbury
Passage translated from the original Latin by George Myerson
An edition of the whole text: Archbishop Anselm, *Proslogium; Monologium: An Appendix in Behalf of the Fool by Gaunilo; and Cur Deus Homo*, edited and translated by Sidney Norton Deane (Chicago, The Open Court Publishing Company) 1903

The Feeling of Inner Strength • Sojourner Truth
As dictated by Sojourner Truth to Olive Gilbert, *Narrative of Sojourner Truth* (Boston, published privately by William Lloyd Garrison for the author) 1850

The Reward of Studying the Stars • Ptolemy
Owen Gingerich, *The Eye of Heaven: Ptolemy, Copernicus, Kepler* (New York, American Institute of Physics) 1993

The Longing to Write • Francesco Petrarca
Francesco Petrarca, *Petrarch, the First Modern Scholar and Man of Letters: A Selection from His Correspondence with Boccaccio and Other Friends, Designed to Illustrate the Beginnings of the Renaissance*, translated by James Harvey Robinson with Henry Winchester Rolfe (New York and London, G. P. Putnam's Sons) 1898

Paternal Praise for a First Novel • Fanny Burney
Fanny Burney, *The Diary and Letters of Frances Burney*, edited by Sarah
Chauncey Woolsey (Boston, Roberts Brothers) 1880

The Lightning Flash of Knowledge • Benjamin Franklin
Benjamin Franklin, *Memoirs of Benjamin Franklin* (Philadelphia, McCarty
and Davis) 1834

The Vitality of Spring • Edward FitzGerald
Edward FitzGerald, *Letters of Edward FitzGerald* (London, Macmillan)
1910

LOVE

The Best Perfume • Elizabeth Barrett
Elizabeth Barrett and Robert Browning, *Letters 1845–46, Vol. 1* (London,
Smith Elder) 1900

A Thousand Kisses • Honoré de Balzac
Honoré de Balzac, *The Love Letters of Honoré de Balzac, 1833–1842*, translated and edited by D. F. Hannigan (London, Downey and Co.) 1901

The Harmony of Souls • John Smith
Albert C. Myers, *Hannah Logan's Courtship* (Philadelphia, Ferris and
Leach) 1904

A Tingling about the Heart • Sydney Owenson
Lady Morgan (Sydney Owenson), *Lady Morgan's Memoirs: Autobiography,
Diaries and Correspondence* (London, William H. Allen) 1862

A Skeptic Has Lost His Head • Leo Tolstoy
Leo Tolstoy, *The Diaries of Leo Tolstoy*, edited by Vladimir Tchertkoff,
translated by C. J. Hogarth and A. Sirnis (London and Toronto, J. M. Dent
& Sons, Ltd.) 1917

Venus Kept Her Promise • Sulpicia
Sulpicia, poem "Tandem venit amor." Translated from the original Latin
by Eleanor Myerson
Text with a translation of the poems as a whole in: James Grainger,
*A Poetical Translation of the Elegies of Tibullus and of the Poems of
Sulpicia* (London, Millar) 1759

A Matchless Face • Richardson Pack
Richardson Pack, "To Clara," in *Poetical Remains* (London, Edmund
Curll) 1738

· Notes ·

The Softness of His Lips • Mary Wollstonecraft
Mary Wollstonecraft, *The Love Letters of Mary Wollstonecraft to Gilbert Imlay*, with a prefatory memoir by Roger Ingpen (London, Hutchinson) 1908

A Comfortable Moment of Communion • Claire de Rémusat
Claire de Rémusat, *Selections from the Letters 1804–13*, translated and edited by Frances Cashel Hoey, John Lillie and Paul de Rémusat (New York, D. Appleton and Company) 1881

Life Surpasses Art • Benjamin Haydon
Benjamin Haydon, *The Life, Letters and Table Talk of Benjamin Robert Haydon*, edited by Richard Henry Stoddard (New York, Scribner, Armstrong & Co.) 1876

EVENING

Moonlight in the Château Garden • Washington Irving
Washington Irving, *The Journals of Washington Irving*, edited by William Trent and George S. Hellman (Boston, The Bibliophile Society) 1919

A Touch of Autumn • Wang Wei
Wang Wei, in *Gems of Chinese Verse*, translated and edited by W. J. B. Fletcher (Shanghai, Commercial Press) 1919

The Music of the Mountain • Hans Christian Andersen
Hans Christian Andersen, *Hans Christian Andersen's Correspondence*, edited by Frederick Crawford (London, Dean and Son) 1891

Books That Bring the Past Alive • Niccolò Machiavelli
Niccolò Machiavelli, *Machiavelli and His Friends: Their Personal Correspondence*, translated and edited by James B. Atkinson and David Sices (DeKalb, Northern Illinois University Press) 1996

A Sense of Beauty as the Sun Sets • Unknown Author
Poem translated from the original Japanese by Alex Dudoq de Wit
Selection from the *Manyoshu* available in *The Sacred Books and Early Literature of the East with an Historical Survey and Descriptions, Vol. 13*, edited by Charles F. Horne (New York, Parke, Austin, and Lipscomb) 1917

The Heart Comes Home to Quietness • Dorothy Wordsworth
Dorothy Wordsworth, *Journals of Dorothy Wordsworth*, edited by William Angus Knight (London, Macmillan & Co.) 1897

A Stroll along the Water • Henri Frédéric Amiel
Henri Frédéric Amiel, *The Journal Intime of Henri-Frédéric Amiel*, translated and edited by Mrs. Humphry Ward (London, Macmillan and Co) 1921

· *Notes* ·

Sweet Calm after a Storm • Francis Higginson
Alexander Young, *Chronicles of the First Planters of the Colony of Massachusetts Bay, from 1623 to 1636* (Boston, Little & Brown) 1846

A Divine Little Book • George Ridpath
George Ridpath, *Diary of George Ridpath, Minister of Stitchel, 1755–1761,* edited by Sir James Balfour Paul (Edinburgh, T. and A. Constable) 1922

At Ease Watching the Boats • Walt Whitman
Walt Whitman, *Diary in Canada, with Extracts from Other of His Diaries and Literary Note-books,* edited by William Sloane Kennedy (Boston, Small, Maynard & Co.) 1904

A Poet's Son Goes to Bed • Ann Yearsley
Ann Yearsley, *The Rural Lyre* (London, C. G. and J. Robinson) 1796

Index